T0247608

Why It's OK
to Not Be
Monogamous

The downsides of monogamy are felt by most people engaged in long-term relationships, including restrictions on self-discovery, limits on friendship, sexual boredom, and a circumscribed understanding of intimacy. Yet, a "happily ever after" monogamy is assumed to be the ideal form of romantic love in many modern societies: a relationship that is morally ideal and will bring the most happiness to its two partners.

In *Why It's OK to Not Be Monogamous*, Justin L. Clardy deeply questions these assumptions. He rejects the claim that non-monogamy among honest, informed and consenting adults is morally impermissible. He shows instead how polyamorous relationships can actually be exemplars of moral virtue. The book discusses how social and political forces sustain and reward monogamous relationships. The book defines non-monogamy as a privative concept; a negation of monogamy. Looking at its prevalence in the United States, the book explains how common criticisms of non-monogamy come up short. Clardy argues, as some researchers have recently shown—monogamy relies on continually demonizing non-monogamy to sustain its moral status. Finally, the book concludes with a focus on equality, asking what justice for polyamorous individuals might look like.

Justin L. Clardy is Assistant Professor of Philosophy at Santa Clara University. He writes on normative questions that emerge in the context of interpersonal relationships and political theories. *Why It's OK to Not Be Monogamous* is Clardy's debut book-length publication.

Why It's OK: The Ethics and Aesthetics of How We Live

Philosophers often build cogent arguments for unpopular positions. Recent examples include cases against marriage and pregnancy, for treating animals as our equals, and dismissing some popular art as aesthetically inferior. What philosophers have done less often is to offer compelling arguments for widespread and established human behavior, like getting married, having children, eating animals, and going to the movies. But if one role for philosophy is to help us reflect on our lives and build sound justifications for our beliefs and actions, it seems odd that philosophers would neglect arguments for the lifestyles most people—including many philosophers—actually lead. Unfortunately, philosophers' inattention to normalcy has meant that the ways of life that define our modern societies have gone largely without defense, even as whole literatures have emerged to condemn them.

Why It's OK: The Ethics and Aesthetics of How We Live seeks to remedy that. It's a series of books that provides accessible, sound, and often new and creative arguments for widespread ethical and aesthetic values. Made up of short volumes that assume no previous knowledge of philosophy from the reader, the series recognizes that philosophy is just as important for understanding what we already believe as it is for criticizing the status quo. The series isn't meant to make us complacent about what we value; rather, it helps and challenges us to think more deeply about the values that give our daily lives meaning.

Titles in Series:

Why It's OK to Make Bad Choices

William Glod

Why It's OK to Enjoy the Work of Immoral Artists

Mary Beth Willard

Why It's OK to Speak Your Mind

Hrishikesh Joshi

Why It's OK to Be a Slacker

Alison Suen

Why It's OK to Eat Meat

Dan C. Shahar

Why It's OK to Love Bad Movies

Matthew Strohl

Why It's OK to Not Be Monogamous

Justin L. Clardy

Selected Forthcoming Titles:

Why It's OK to Mind Your Own Business

Justin Tosi and Brandon Warmke

Why It's OK to Be Fat

Rekha Nath

Why It's OK to Be a Socialist

Christine Sypnowich

Why It's OK to Be a Moral Failure

Robert B. Talisse

For further information about this series, please visit: www.routledge.com/
Why-Its-OK/book-series/WIOK

JUSTIN L. CLARDY

Why It's OK
to Not Be
Monogamous

Routledge
Taylor & Francis Group
NEW YORK AND LONDON

Designed cover image: Andy Goodman

First published 2023
by Routledge
605 Third Avenue, New York, NY 10158

and by Routledge
4 Park Square, Milton Park, Abingdon, Oxon, OX14 4RN

Routledge is an imprint of the Taylor & Francis Group, an informa business

© 2023 Taylor & Francis

ISBN: 978-1-032-45019-3 (hbk)
ISBN: 978-1-032-44978-4 (pbk)
ISBN: 978-1-003-37503-6 (ebk)

DOI: 10.4324/9781003375036

Typeset in Joanna MT Pro and DIN pro
by Newgen Publishing UK

For my late mother, Bonnie Wallace;
and my beloved son, Josiah.

For my relata, past and present.

Contents

Acknowledgments

Writing a book is always a challenging undertaking and can be an isolating process. For me, this was made even more so as the project had to be carried out shortly after the loss of my mother and amidst a global health pandemic. While I am the book's only author, I am grateful that I did not have to write this book alone.

I am grateful for my position in the department of Philosophy at Santa Clara University, where I benefit from a congenial philosophical environment and overwhelming support from my colleagues in carrying out this work. I would like to extend particular thanks to the organizing committee of the department's Prior conference where I was able to present parts of this project in their very early stages. I am also pleased that my posts at both Santa Clara University and Stanford University put me in conversation with talented undergraduates whose innovation and ingenuity inspired me regularly. Thank you.

I am extremely thankful for my tight-knit group of Black colleagues at Santa Clara as well. While many of you arrived on campus toward the tail-end of this project, you have all been a source of critical strength and support for me professionally and socially. I would like my readership to also know that at the time of this writing, I am still undefeated in our Spades group. Don't @ me. I love you all, and thank you.

Portions of this book were presented in a series of invited talks at various venues including the University of Tampa, Pepperdine University, and the Poly Cultural Diversity Alliance, where audiences found use in what I was doing and offered helpful feedback in giving this book its shape. Thank you.

I have been extremely fortunate to have had opportunities for my work to appear in popular media outlets including *Life on the Swingset Podcast*, *Spectrum* by Jubilee, *The Tamron Hall Show*, KJLH's *The Love Zone Podcast*, the KBLA 1580am talk radio show *Let's Get Intimate*, the *Normalizing Non-Monogamy Podcast*, and *The UnMute Podcast* with Myisha Cherry. I am grateful for invitations from these platforms to talk about love, non-monogamy, and polyamory. Not only have they increased my work's public visibility, they have also been instrumental in moving discussions about non-monogamy and polyamory into the mainstream. Thank you.

In writing this book, there were times where I felt lost in my arguments and did not have the privilege of setting up short chats with friends and colleagues to help me work through my thoughts as I would have prior to COVID-19. In these times I turned to my personal blog on *Medium* to get some of the ideas and arguments out. To this end, I am also enormously grateful for the members of my audience who took time to engage with those arguments. Your engagement was crucial in keeping me going. Thank you.

I received pertinent and helpful conversations, comments, and suggestions on early drafts from Michelle Mueller, Harry Chalmers, Luke Bruninng, Zach Biondi, anonymous reviewers, and from the editing team at Routledge. Thank you.

This project would not have been possible without the support of my family and friends. I am thankful for everyone that I came into contact with while writing this project. I am not exaggerating when I write that I have learned something from you all. This is the part that makes acknowledgment sections extremely difficult to write; people will inevitably be left out. Still there are some who I do wish to take the space to explicitly recognize as I ask for grace in advance if there are omissions.

Thank you to Mason Marshall. You are the one who introduced me to the field that I would inevitably make a career from—Philosophy of Love—so many years ago. You nurtured my early philosophical thought on these matters and empowered me to continue pursuing truth about a phenomenon so many philosophers find okay to ignore. You told me my questions were both meaningful and important and I will always thank you for that. Similarly, I extend thanks to Eric Funkhouser, Warren Herold, and Oksana Maksymchuk for helping me hone my skills as a writer in philosophy.

Thank you to the wonderful staff at Coffee & Water Lab. It was not easy to find a new local coffee shop in the south Bay Area that suited my writing needs in the middle of a pandemic. You all were reliably open in the wee hours of the morning, where I would get most of my writing done. You all took the time to learn my name and my "regular" order— yup, that good ole *lavender fog*! Thank you for the delightful conversations, hospitality, vibey music, and the occasional drink on the house. (I promise to pay you back for those when this book makes it big! Just kidding.) I truly feel like my business is appreciated. The Lab became my home away from home; my writing nook away from my writing nook. Thank you.

Thank you to my relata. You all helped me see through some of the tougher times that this project presented. You reminded me to eat and you ate with and fed me; you reminded me to leave my house; to watch movies and shows (and did it with me); to go see live music. You helped keep me afloat financially. You encouraged me to keep to my yoga practice; to jog and run a half marathon. You cracked jokes about me and the culture. You talked with me and never let me take myself too seriously. You celebrated the milestones and shared the frustrations. You reminded me to write and wrote with me. You accompanied me whitewater rafting. After my bike accident, you nursed me and told me that I "gotta get back on the bike, at some point" and I doubt if wiser words have ever been spoken. Above all, you've loved me through extended periods of inconsistent communication and have been my joy and peace throughout this process. I love each of you dearly. Thank you.

To the homie Kevin Morris, I appreciate you for holding a brutha down and talking hoops and a bunch of other random stuff with the boy. Thank you.

To my sisters Jasmin and Jordan, you two are my backbones and I cannot imagine a world where I have two better siblings. I am tremendously proud of the Black women you are both becoming. Our countless conversations about everything from internet memes to Insecure or Euphoria or what's on our go-to playlists at any given time, all give me life, okayyy! You both sometimes come to me for relationship advice hoping that I might have some insight to impart. I am sorry to disappoint you more times than not, but I am usually the one learning more about love and relationships through yall's lenses. I have wanted nothing more for your intimate lives but for them to be empowering and autonomous and yall have been wearing it well. Thank you for your love (and for visiting me to keep me company as often as you did).

To my Dad, thank you for talking with me almost every day and for your endless wisdom on, well, just about anything really; a true "Jack" of all trades. (Do you see what I did there?) To my Grandmother and her unconditional love of a knucklehead like me. Thank you for introducing me to the pleasure of reading and doing it critically. To my Granny, for the warm hospitality whenever I need it. Last, but certainly not least, to my son, for being perfectly clever and quick-witted, always keeping me on my toes and laughing hard at me when I flounder. You are most brilliant, black child. (Thanks also to your mother for backing me on this point.)

Acknowledgments

Ethical non-monogamy is not a new phenomenon.

But over the last ten years, discussion of it has entered public discourse more widely. Increasing numbers of legal and political theorists and philosophers have argued that current family law and dominant social norms fail to recognize the wide variety of intimate personal relationships in which humans can thrive. While some have worried that same-sex marriage would open the door to polygamous marriage, others have asked, why not recognize and support all caregiving relationships between consenting adults, whether they involve two people—or more?

We can meet our needs for love and care in many different configurations and relationship types. Yet social norms assume that one relationship type, the romantic sexual dyad, will fit all of us. Marriage law likewise recognizes only two-person relationships. These constraints are harmful if they prevent people from entering relationships which would be more fulfilling to them or keep them in relationships which cause unhappiness. They are also harmful if they perpetuate damaging stigmas against relationship non-conformists.

Stigma against non-monogamists produces real harms: non-monogamists can lose their jobs, housing, even child custody. (And this is not to mention the misunderstandings and stigma encountered by asexuals, aromantics, and those who simply prefer not to be in romantic and sexual relationships.)

For some people, such stigma against non-monogamists is justified because, they believe, non-monogamy is immoral—it's not OK, morally speaking. Of course, *some* forms of non-monogamy are immoral—such as any cases involving coercion, significant power inequality between the parties, dishonest or manipulative seduction, or lack of consideration for partners' feelings. But of course, monogamy can involve all of those features too.

As Justin Clardy points out in this incisive treatise, we cannot interrogate non-monogamy without interrogating monogamy. Too often, arguments against non-monogamy focus on the worst cases of non-monogamy while contrasting them with the best cases of monogamy, conveniently ignoring abusive monogamous relationships and the history of coverture.

If, as Clardy suggests, we focus on the *best* cases of non-monogamy, such as egalitarian and consensual forms of polyamory, what those who object to non-monogamy object to is simply the practice of having multiple sexual partners. This book promises an argument that non-monogamy, specifically, polyamory, is OK. Indeed, it goes further than advertised to ask: is polyamory not just permissible, but just as good, ethically speaking, as monogamy?

Consider how monogamy is prized. Monogamists are privileged by law and social norms. To be married, and therefore, in most places, presumed monogamous, still carries an unearned presumption of responsibility and even virtue. Having multiple partners is, by contrast, too often presumed to mean that someone hasn't found the right *one* for them yet or else that they are incapable of love and commitment.

But why must love and commitment in a romantic and sexual relationship be to just one person? If love and commitment are goods, is there something to be said for seeking them with more people, rather than fewer, if the others are similarly inclined?

It is worth pausing to ask, as Amia Srinivasan charges us in *The Right to Sex*, what social and political forces have shaped our sexual desires and practices.[1] If monogamy and mononormativity are a relic of settler colonialism, as Kim TallBear argues, can non-monogamy be liberatory?[2] If they are an instrument of capitalism, as Friedrich Engels and Emma Goldman suggest, would it benefit us individually and collectively to adopt less possessive norms of relationship?[3] What interests are served by mononormativity—and what might a more pluralistic culture of relationships make possible? For example, could polyamorous co-housing be a response to rising housing prices—and polyamorous co-parenting a response to increase demands on working parents? What if we all sought more love instead of more money? Or allowed our relationships to be fluid, without rushing to define them or fit them into a preconceived progression?

In this book, Justin Clardy brings together moral and political philosophy and philosophy of sex and emotions with writings from poly sub-cultures to create a heady mix of ideas, never deviating from his cogent main line of argument. He addresses the full range of questions you might have about non-monogamy: What are monogamy, non-monogamy, and polyamory? Are there any compelling arguments for monogamy or against non-monogamy? And what does society owe to polyamorists?

This is not a mere academic exercise; it touches on some of the most important things in life. As Clardy writes in Chapter 2, "Love and loving relationships are serious matters." Loving relationships are among the great goods of life; they define our identity, support our mental health and self-esteem (when they are good), and can provide us with affection, care, and companionship. If it is possible, indeed, permissible, to have more of them—isn't this something worth knowing, perhaps as a matter of urgency?

This book leads the reader through the strongest arguments on both sides of the debate in a highly accessible and engaging way. It will make even the skeptical reader think deeply about these timely questions.

In recent years, discussions of love have been changing. In 2020, a city council in Sommerville, Massachusetts decided to grant polyamorous people rights that are typically held by spouses in a marriage. In 2021, Cambridge, Massachusetts became the second city to do so. At a social level, relationships that are, at least arguably, "ethically" non-monogamous are more apparent. These portrayals are becoming more diverse as they move into the mainstream as well. Beyond HBO's *Big Love* series (which depicted white, middle-class, Mormon polygamists), non-monogamous relationships have been featured in Netflix's *She's Gotta Have it*, Facebook's *The Red Table Talk*, HBO's *Insecure* and *Trigonometry*, and Starz's *Power*, many of which feature primarily Black casts. Polyamorous relationships are also on the rise. It is estimated that between 4–5% of the U.S. population is currently involved in consensually non-monogamous relationships. Dating apps, such as *Feeld* and *Open*, have been developed to cater to a growing non-monogamous demographic in the dating market. And three gay polyamorous men in California fought to have all of their names enlisted on their child's birth certificate and won. At the present moment, more people are asking if it is okay to not be monogamous.

DOI: 10.4324/9781003375036-1

In America, and many other places throughout the world, monogamous romantic love relationships are prestigious. They're an "achievement", so to speak. People often congratulate their loved ones when they get news of engagements to be married. This is understandable. Monogamy takes up much space in our discussions about love; after all, it is the more prominent and socially acceptable form of romantic relationship. Feminist philosopher Elizabeth Brake has pointed out that in the United States, marriage is backed by a powerful industrial complex that propagandizes the "married couple" as a goal for everyone. We are told at every corner that loving correctly, is to love monogamously—with one person at a time. From an early age, we are conditioned to think about love in a straight line. First comes love; then comes marriage; then comes a baby in the baby carriage. Presently, only monogamous relationships are protected by marriage. If romantic relationships aim at marriage, then, they also aim at monogamy.

Marriage (and marriage-like) relationships control the "love story" so to speak both personally and socially. In other words, monogamous ideologies dominate discourses about love, and these ideologies are reproduced in everyday conversations and mainstream media depictions. Thinking that it's "ok" to be non-monogamous is uncommon. Many people ask whether it's *possible*, let alone practical, to be in multiple relationships at the same time. Even among those who accept the possibility of non-monogamous love, it may still strike them as "odd", to say the least. They wonder, puzzledly, "How does it work?"

There have been many self-help books that respond to this question. Dossie Easton's *The Ethical Slut* was among the early wave of popular books on "ethical non-monogamy" or "consensual non-monogamy". Since the publication of Easton's work, there has been an outpouring of work that aims to show people how non-monogamy works. For example, there's Tamara Pincus' *It's Called "Polyamory": Coming Out About Your Nonmonogamous Relationships*, Jessica Fern's *Polysecure: Attachment, Trauma and Consensual Nonmonogamy*, and Mark A. Michaels and Patricia Johnson's *Designer Relationships: A guide to happy monogamy, positive polyamory, and optimistic open relationships*. Many of these books, however, assume the validity of non-monogamous relationships and do not make critical arguments about their ethicality.

In the last two decades, research on non-monogamies has been expanding, but theorizing about non-monogamies is still a fairly recent endeavor in the philosophy of love. Thinking about non-monogamies has given rise to an unchartered frontier of thought. We are on the precipice of new discoveries about love and relationships; we are asking new and more challenging questions about them. For example, Pepper Mint discusses the necessary relationship between monogamy on the one hand, and the non-monogamies "cheating" and "adultery," on the other, arguing that monogamy relies on these non-monogamies in fundamental ways. Nathan Rambukkana has introduced the concept of "non/monogamy" to help us better understand how both monogamous and non-monogamous relationships are a part of a single system that distributes powers and privilege to some intimate relationships, but not to others. He argues that monogamies and non-monogamies are a part of the same spectrum of intimate relationships and that they are two sides of the same socio-cultural coin. Philosophical work by Carrie Jenkins has pointed out pernicious assumptions made about different modes of intimate relationships. Patricia Marino's *The Philosophy of Sex and Love: An Opinionated Introduction* has a fine chapter on ethical non-monogamy as well. Volumes and Special issues of academic journals focusing on non-monogamy have been published too. For example, Meg Barker and Langdridge's *Understanding Non-Monogamies* and the *Journal of Black Sexuality's* issue on polyamory are impressive collections of interdisciplinary work on non-monogamous relationships. Important works that feature non-monogamies also aim at marriage and the need to reform or abolish it. Ronald Den Otter's *Plural Marriage* or Elizabeth Brake's *After Marriage* and *Minimizing Marriage* are fine examples. In some of my previous work, I have also attempted to carve out a lane among critics of monogamies and non-monogamies. These thinkers are all doing pioneering work that cannot be overlooked. Their efforts to pursue new truths and understandings about love, along with the likes of scholars such as Ann Tweedy, Elizabeth Sheff, Harry Chalmers, and Luke Brunning, should be admired and revered. They have been instrumental in establishing a basis for thinking critically about non-monogamous love and the social & political station of non-monogamous people—such as *polyamorists*, or people who believe it is okay to have more than one romantic relationship at the same time with the knowledge and consent of all of the relata involved.

Calling attention to the social and political realities that non-monogamous people face is perhaps one of the things to admire most about non-monogamous theory. Unlike narratives of love and romance rooted in fantastical fiction, they situate our intimate relationships in our actual world. These thinkers have put a spotlight on under-discussed systems of oppression such as *amatonormativity* (i.e., the belief that a central, dyadic romantic relationship that leads to marriage is the ideal romantic relationship, a universally shared goal, and should be pursued above all other relationships) and mononormativity (i.e., the dominant narratives of monogamy and monogamous relationships that appear in mass media and everyday conversations) to uncover the injustices that polyamorists face, for example. Polyamorists have been fired (or not hired), denied housing, denied citizenship, denied participation in marriage, had their families broken up, and have been legally prosecuted based on their polyamorous identities and lifestyles. These systems are a pervasive normative force in the United States that interlock in ways that perniciously discriminate against, marginalize, and oppress polyamorists.

If it is permissible to be polyamorous, then it may not be okay to sit idly by while these forces are oppressing minority groups of people. Existing work on polyamory and other non-monogamies sometimes takes their moral standing for granted as the language of "ethical non-monogamy" or "consensual non-monogamy" tends to show. Ethical or consensual non-monogamists distinguish themselves from cheaters and adulterers. However, appealing to consent as some kind of "moral magic" that transforms otherwise unethical relationships into ethical ones, has not thoroughly been interrogated. Scholars have asked about the harmfulness of jealousy and of our practical limits as humans (such as having limited time, energy, or attention), for example, and less about what consent might mean for a group and whether such consent can be established. Does group consent create unique challenges for privacy? Beyond one's individual preferences, is polyamory, on the whole, detrimental to the fabric of society?

This book argues that it is okay (read as, morally permissible) to not be monogamous. Highlighting a variety of non-monogamies, including polyamory, friendship, and singledom, the book examines the common (and not so common) reasons for thinking non-monogamies are not, in fact, morally permissible. If there are unique moral challenges that non-monogamies cannot meet, we might have overwhelming reasons to reject them. Specifically, this book picks out polyamorous relationships as an exemplary form of non-monogamy that is, at the very least, ethically permissible, if not preferable. I make use of Rambukkana's non/monogamy device to place intimate relationships on the same spectrum. I argue that non/monogamy helps us understand how the belief that monogamy is morally permissible hinges on demonizing non-monogamies. The comparisons between monogamy and cheating, for example, are made possible through the non/monogamy spectrum. Finally, my argument shows that polyamory's permissibility entails consequences for liberal societies. For example, if being non-monogamous is okay, it is not just for liberal states to routinely discriminate against and fail to recognize these intimate relationships and the relata that constitute them. This work urges that liberal societies have a responsibility to expand the institution of marriage to include multi-party unions.

The arguments unfold over four chapters. Chapter 1 looks at monogamy and non-monogamy. What is monogamy and non-monogamy? Many of the questions that bear on non-monogamy also bear on monogamy. Despite the assumption that "We all know what monogamy means," the essence of monogamy can be quite elusive. This chapter draws on recent literature in the Philosophy of Love that addresses both the metaphysical and ethical status of monogamies and non-monogamies. It argues that monogamy is a social convention and that non-monogamy is a negation of this convention involving the rejection of the normative belief that romantic or sexual relationships must be between two and only two people at a time. Spanning across a variety of intimacies including adultery, cheating, swinging, and polyfidelity, I pick out polyamory as a morally exemplary form of non-monogamy. Finally, the chapter demonstrates how social and political forces converge to create and sustain normative pressure—mononormativity—that prioritizes and rewards monogamous relationships.

Chapter 2 advances the case for why it is ok to be non-monogamous by showing how the common arguments defending monogamy's moral standing can be rejected in some cases and, in others, be extended to non-monogamies. The chapter focuses on polyamory and defends its status as morally permissible. In doing so, it also addresses some of the more common objections to non-monogamy including naturalism, divine ordination, the TEA objection, specialness, sexual health, and jealousy. Some have cursed non-monogamous behavior because they believe that monogamous relationships are ordained by God as the only moral form of romantic relationship. More recently, other scholars have offered more interesting proposals that the chapter investigates such as concerns over consent, privacy, agency, power distribution in romantic relationships, gendered asymmetries, and polyamorous families. I argue against thinking that polyamory erodes a society's fabric and instead point to ways that it might have the opposite effect. Additionally, the chapter foregrounds how monogamy is politicized in public discourse around romantic love and relationships in ways that perpetually marginalize non-monogamists, and especially polyamorists.

Chapter 3 looks at monogamous and non-monogamous identity. Some people ask whether monogamy and non-monogamies are identities or practices. Are people simply "born that way"? For many people, monogamy and non-monogamy are beyond something that they *do* rather it is *who they are*. This chapter works through a schema for understanding monogamous and non-monogamous identity that centralizes a kind of ideological embeddedness and resonance. The chapter contrasts the socially constructed nature of relational identities against the view that relational identities are *essential* to a person.

Chapter 4 places polyamory in a larger conversation about rights and social injustice. Shifting from metaphysical and moral discussions about non-monogamy to thinking about the treatment of polyamorists in society at large, it addresses questions such as how the institution of marriage factors into polyamorous marginalization, exclusion, and violence. Are polyamorists a political group? Furthermore, are they worthy of special protections under the law? Broadly speaking, what might "justice for polyamorists" look like? This chapter argues that amatonormativity and mononormativity are free-standing systems of oppression that routinely marginalize polyamorous people. It argues that asking questions about the political consequences and impact on polyamorous relationships is an urgent matter.

I wish to make note of a few things involving the book's language before proceeding. I realize that thinking about non-monogamy is new and challenging for many people. As Ani Ritchie and Meg Barker's work has shown, communities of non-monogamists have had to develop their own languages to describe who they are and how they feel. As a result, much of the language and terminology needed to discuss the ethical dimensions of polyamory may seem technical and unnecessary. However, I believe that preserving as much of the language that these communities use to describe themselves and their experiences marks the kind of academic integrity that is a hallmark of good research. This means that in many places throughout this book, I have made choices to preserve this integrity and sometimes at the expense of ease to inexperienced readers. However, these same readers should be encouraged to understand non-monogamists on their own terms; though it may be slightly more laborious, it can be extremely rewarding. To be somewhat helpful, though, I wish to make a few stipulations for terminological choices that were made for the sake of clarity, precision, and overall reduction of labor for the reader.

I make use of the term *relata* often to describe the parties that make up romantic relationships. The term relata is useful for discussing polyamorous romantic relationships in ways that avoid problematic assumptions about gender and number. Relata may appropriately refer to men, women, romantic dyads, or multi-party romantic relationships alike. I use the term "extrarelational" and its associated variants to refer to relationships that extend from or exist alongside dyadic romantic relationships. As such, polyamorous relationships necessarily have extrarelational relationships in ways that monogamous relationships need not. When I speak of love in this book, I am referring to romantic love as it exists in the context of the contemporary United States and in places that are sufficiently culturally similar. In many ways, romantic love is a socio-cultural construction, and beliefs about the phenomenon and its acceptable practices will vary from culture to culture so it is important to point this out. At base, along with thinkers like Niko Kolodny, Diane Jeske, and others, I take romantic love to be a reason-responsive emotion that involves a final valuation of a relationship, from the perspective of relata in that relationship, and nonfinal noninstrumental valuation of one's relata. I have also chosen to italicize *non/monogamy* (and *non/monogamous*) when directly referencing the conceptual tool developed by Rambukkana to describe the landscape of intimate relationships. When I make reference to some particular instance of a non-monogamous relationship, I index this with the hyphen and it is not italicized. And finally, I do not assume that love necessarily bears any special connection to sex or marriage. Therefore, any associations of sex and marriage with love throughout this work should be understood as nonessential.

Readers should keep in mind that this book does not intend to be a self-help book of any variety. Instead, it is a philosophical inquiry that delves into the moral status of non-monogamy. It offers a set of arguments that seek to establish that non-monogamy, but more specifically, polyamory, is ethically permissible. As scholarship on non-monogamy is growing, in the Philosophy of Love, in particular, its presence is still sparse. As a result, in addition to considering the more prominent arguments that come from the philosophy of love, the arguments contained in this book also rely on insights from legal theory, political science, political theory, queer studies, women and gender studies, sociology, feminist theory, political theory, and history. Where appropriate, I make use of examples of romantic relationships from popular media such as television, movies, novels, and songs. Overall, this book invites readers to pause and think critically about the alternatives to monogamy and about monogamy itself. It is to this inquiry that we may now turn.

One

INTRODUCTION

Sadly, it is not possible to talk about non-monogamy without talking about monogamy. Monogamy's embeddedness in Western culture can make its pervasiveness hard to see. Cloaked in discussions about romantic love, monogamy can pull off quite the masquerade—that is, it often gets disguised as love itself. After all, many people still believe in "traditional" marriage and want to get married for reasons they believe are rooted firmly in love. Since, at the time of this writing, marriage in the United States by and large exists to protect intimate dyads (relationships with two and only two people),[1] a desire for marriage is often an implicit desire for a particular kind of romantic relationship—namely a monogamous one. But what exactly *is* monogamy and what is its relationship to romantic love? Despite the assumption that "we all know what monogamy means", the essence of monogamy is quite elusive. Is it an identity? Is it a relationship style or practice? Is it an ideology? Do time, space, and simultaneity have anything to do with it? Does marriage? Is it possible for monogamous people to have threesomes? And what might it mean for monogamy that more and more people are experimenting with and participating in loving romantic

DOI: 10.4324/9781003375036-2

relationships that are consensually non-monogamous?[2] For some readers, this chapter may "spoil the party", so to speak, by disambiguating these questions and lifting the mask of love from monogamy's face.

Monogamy can be insidious. Many philosophical discussions of romantic love include an unargued assumption that the only metaphysically possible romantic love relationships are monogamous ones.[3] This presumption is so widespread that it often appears without defense or comment.

Over the last five decades, there has been a significant rise in academic research focusing on non-monogamy. People have asked what is non-monogamy and how does it work? In this chapter, I argue that non-monogamy is the negation of monogamy, characterized by the belief that monogamous relationships are not the only valuable form of intimate or romantic relationships. I draw on Nathan Rambukkana's concept of non/monogamy to establish the parameters for understanding what non-monogamy is. This concept creates the landscape for a range of intimate relationships that are both conceivable and worth having.

The non/monogamy spectrum situates monogamous intimacies on the same spectrum as non-monogamous intimacies. Understanding how intimate relationships function along this spectrum is useful for determining whether some non-monogamies, if any, are more or less privileged or transformative than other non-monogamies. Are open polyamorous relationships as privileged as their polyfidelitous counterparts? The same can be said for adjudicating the ethicality of different non-monogamous intimacies. Are consensual non-monogamous relationships ethically permissible? These are questions that the latter part of this chapter addresses. For now, I turn our attention to the question of monogamy, before moving to its negation.

WHAT IS MONOGAMY?

As an opening remark, it is worth noting that historically, "monogamy" has meant various things. For example, John McMurtry writes that "*The number of partners involved in the marriage must be two and only two* (as opposed to three, four, five, or any of the countless other possibilities of intimate union)."[4] In contemporary Western societies, however, monogamy is extended far beyond this narrow meaning. We speak of monogamous relationships between unmarried persons and of aspirational monogamous relationships (as the social media hashtag #RelationshipGoals or many dating profiles are likely to suggest). Some single people who are looking to date readily declare that they *are* monogamous, too. It is the wider use of monogamy that concerns us here. I suggest that monogamy is, at its base, a social convention that centralizes dyadic relationships. Additionally, I maintain that monogamous relationships have particular intimacy confining constraints as a hallmark—namely, they are romantically exclusive. I take *romantic exclusivity* to involve a combination of both sexual and emotional exclusivity. This stipulative definition of exclusivity is careful to refer beyond merely refraining from sexual activity with others. The American Association for Marriage and Family Therapy discusses a "new crisis of infidelity" in the age of social media and technology called "emotional affairs". So, while sex with others can compromise the integrity of monogamous relationships, a variety of non-sexual involvements can too.[5] Any understanding of monogamy that focuses on sexual restrictions *only* is thereby not sufficiently inclusive.

These preliminary remarks are about scope. A satisfactory understanding of monogamy will be appropriately wide enough in scope to accommodate 'monogamous' singles, unmarried couples that are in marriage-like relationships, and a range of non-sexual involvements. After all, non-monogamous relationships can also be governed by a kind of romantic exclusivity (i.e., polyfidels), despite having more than two relata.[6] So, while monogamists expect romantic exclusivity, they do not do so *exclusively*. Romantic exclusivity, in other words, is not reserved for monogamy. This uncovers an important feature of monogamy, namely that monogamous relationships are *dyadic*—that is, they are between two and only two people at a time. The reference to time—i.e., "at a time"—has implications for love. Those who are committed to the view that monogamous love lasts a lifetime imply that an individual can have only one true love over a single lifetime.[7] Monogamy as I've been describing it is not as strong. In stating that monogamy's dyadic condition is temporaneous, we take for granted that people can have multiple loves throughout a single life, so long as those loves were dyadic at the time that the romantic relationship existed.

Temporal concerns aside, monogamous logics usually appeal to something about a relationship's structure or form. As Diane Enns and Niko Kolodny rightly recognize, most of the time, discussions about love *just are* discussions about relationships.[8] However, even people who are not in romantic relationships still claim that they are monogamous. But how can this be? The fact that, for many, monogamy is something far dearer to them than a mere relationship style, prompts us to ask the question of whether monogamy might be an identity. If so, what kind? A sexual identity? A romantic one? A satisfactory understanding of monogamy will also be able to speak to these concerns.

MONOGAMY AS A SOCIAL CONVENTION

On my view, monogamy is a social convention. In part, this is to say that monogamy involves a particular collection of conventional beliefs about human relationships. This section will help clarify the set of beliefs that non-monogamy negates. In the strictest sense, monogamy includes the following beliefs:

i.   Romantic relationships are attitude-dependent
ii. Romantic relationships are dyadic
iii. Romantic relationships are emotionally exclusive
iv. Romantic relationships are sexually exclusive

There is plenty to unpack here. First, what exactly is a relationship? Niko Kolodny reminds us that "not every interpersonal relation, … is an interpersonal relationship in the sense in which relations between friends, lovers, and family members are relationships."[9] Romantic relationships are distinct in our social ontology. They are accumulations of shared activities that persist between *particular people* over time. The fact that shared activities (e.g., spending time together, talking with one another, having sex, etc.) in relationships are accumulative also points to another feature of relationships—specifically, that they are *historical*; in other words, "whether I stand in a relationship to someone at a given time depends on some fact about our pasts."[10] So, there will be some historical pattern of attitudes and actions between the relata.

Relationships are also attitude-dependent. Whether or not relata have a particular relationship of some kind (e.g., friendship, romantic relationship, etc.) depends on a sharedness in attitude between the relata—the relata will agree about (if asked) whether or not they have some particular kind of relationship or another. When Mal is asked whether they have a romantic relationship with Zed, we should expect that Mal's response will also be echoed by Zed themselves. Otherwise, we should perhaps suspect that Mal is delusional and this is troubling.

So, relationships are attitude-dependent, ongoing, with particular people, and historical. This is true for friendships as much as romantic relationships. Yet for all we have said about relationships so far, we have not yet zeroed in on monogamous *romantic* relationships.

Romantic Relationships are Dyadic

Of monogamy's constitutive beliefs, (ii.) says that romantic relationships are dyadic. Hidalgo and colleagues introduce a helpful notion that they call the *dyadic imaginary*. The dyadic imaginary can be thought of as the surrounding ideology in love discourse that legitimate romantic relationships are between two and only two people at a time. Within the imaginary, the dyad is the standard for legitimate and prescriptive sociosexual arrangements.[11] As "The couple relationship is traditionally central to our understanding of love and intimacy in families [in the West]," the dyad is centered and prioritized in how we understand not only romantic love but also romantic relationships.[12] The couple thereby is the dominant image for love-talk permeated throughout society. For example, epic romance films such as *Titanic* or *The Notebook* are about dyadic romantic relationships. Furthermore, marriage is still, by and large, looked upon as the goal for which all romantic relationships aim.

Judith Butler urges that the "dyad is an achievement, not a presupposition."[13] Butler situates human relationships in a landscape of social processes that transform important realities about the self. From Butler's vantage point, then, dyadism is not a metaphysical presupposition, but an "achievement". Here, however, I urge that dyadism *is* a social and political presupposition in the U.S.

The terms *amatonormativity* and *mononormativity* have been introduced by love scholars to explain how the dyadic imaginary is propped up. They maintain that these normativities aim to sustain monogamy and that they create normative social pressure with oppressive effects. Emerging from the first International Conference on Polyamory and Mononormativity held at the Research Centre for Feminist, Gender and Queer Studies at the University of Hamburg in 2005, the coining of the term "mononormativity" belongs to Robin Bauer and Marianne Pieper. As Ani Ritchie and Meg Barker have explained, mononormativity is the dominant discourse of monogamy which is reproduced and perpetuated in everyday conversation and saturates mainstream media depictions.[14] In *Minimizing Marriage*, Elizabeth Brake coined the term "amatonormativity" to describe the assumption that a central, exclusive, romantic relationship is normal for humans, and a goal all humans share. Such a relationship is normative in the sense that it *should* be aimed at in preference to other relationship types.[15] Each of these normative forces treats the romantic dyad centrally and reinforces the thought that romantic relationships are composed of two and only two relata.

Amatonormativity and mononormativity function in ways that shape and control the narratives we tell ourselves about romantic love and intimate relationships. These norms are apparent in wedding-industrial complexes that broadcast propaganda centralizing dyads in books, magazines, songs, advertising, television shows, and movies.[16] People long to find their "one true love" or their "Mr. or Ms. Right" and aim to stay together forever. When non-dyadic relationships make appearances in media, they are often portrayed as threats to their more respectable dyadic counterparts—i.e., through the lens of cheating or infidelities. Mimi Schippers and Pepper Mint have pointed out that monogamy *fundamentally* needs cheating.[17] Elsewhere, I have argued that narratives of non-dyadic infidelities are important mechanisms for sustaining mononormativity and amatonormativity as unscathed hegemonic norms.[18] Through subterfuge, infidelity (understood as monogamy's non-dyadic diabolical opposite), functions to compel people to conform to dyadic norms and discourage participation in intimate relationships with more than two people such as polyamory or other forms of consensual non-monogamy.

One might think that infidelity does not serve our purposes here. It might be said that infidelity does not track numbers. Insofar as it violates a commitment of fidelity it is a violation of a relational rule (potentially having nothing to do with number). For example, the relata in closed polyamorous relationships of more than two people can "cheat" even though their relationship is non-dyadic.[19] The point here though is that in the dyadic imaginary, infidelity violates monogamy precisely because monogamous relationships are supposed to be dyadic. Cheating is deplorable in the monogamous imagination simply because of its negation of the idealistic dyad; it is non-dyadic. Because monogamous relationships are normative in mononormative societies, it is infidelity's negation of the dyad which enables judgments of character deficiencies cheaters are said to have. So, while it may be the case that the dyad is a *metaphysical* achievement rather than a presupposition, socially and politically throughout the U.S. it is the dominant presupposition in discourses about love and romance.

Romantic Relationships and their Exclusivities

Other components of monogamy involve the exclusivities that characterize it. Couples regularly substantiate their monogamies through terms of sexual, emotional, and/or romantic exclusivity to preserve their already limited time, energy, and attention; or to feel "special". In effect, people believe these exclusivities protect the dyadic relationship by restricting important relational resources to the members of the dyad—particularly sexual and/or emotional resources. It is important to note that practitioners of monogamy take different approaches to exclusivity. Some vie for an exclusive investment of resources that are not sexual and emotional, such as money or other capital. In other cases, emotional resources are of higher priority than sexual ones. This is why Meg Barker, Nathan Rambukkana, and others utilize the suffix "-ies" when discussing monogamies and non-monogamies.[20] The plural suffix of "-ies" foregrounds the variation that we find among these ways of relating.

Generally speaking, monogamy requires what I call romantic exclusivity—or the combination of both emotional and sexual exclusivity. As I mentioned above, sexual and emotional exclusivity may come apart. I also concede that some relationships which require either emotional or sexual exclusivity, might be legibly understood as "monogamous". More to come on this later.

Emotional exclusivity requires that relata restrict the formation of relationships that mimic the intimacy or emotional closeness in one's romantic relationship. According to the American Association for Marriage and Family Therapy, emotional affairs have been cited as a growing contributor to divorce in American marriages.[21] For some lovers, emotional affairs are important and threaten the integrity of one's romantic relationship.[22] The alleged threat has to do with emotional affairs being associated with the consideration of a romantic commitment with the person that the emotional affair is with.

Emotional exclusivity might be desired for different reasons. One reason is that emotional intimacy is a good of romantic relationships. Being close to our partners helps us feel safe and secure. In addition to romantic relationships being structured by complex webs of expectations, memories, care, and trust, they are also characterized by the intimate experiences that we share with our partners. They involve frequent intimate self-disclosures among relata. As Gary Chartier remarks on the intimacy achieved within dyadic relationships:

> A couple's relationship is itself the prime (albeit not exclusive) goal of their conversation... Talking is not everything but it is essential. And one must not only volunteer one's own thoughts and feelings; One must also seek actively to elicit the thoughts and feelings of the other with questions and responses that make clear that one is interested in the experiences, perspectives, and

memories of one's partner and that one seeks persistently to understand them.[23]

In an important sense, our mouths are windows to ourselves. Self-disclosures to our partners both create and reinforce the basis for intimacy between the relata; enabling them to close in on one another or otherwise deepen their relationship. When the parties to the relationship begin to regularly share more of themselves than is socially customary and within a context of caring with someone else, this may threaten the potential for fostering optimal intimacy in the primary or formal dyadic romantic relationship. The insecurity that often results can be harmful to some relata.[24]

In addition to threatening intimacy in the relationship, people like to feel special in their romantic relationships. They like to feel not only that they are unique in their own right, but also that they are in a relationally unique relationship. When one participates in dyadic monogamous relationships, this choice simultaneously signifies that the relata are choosing one another to relate to (above all other viable candidates for partnership). This is what supports the idea of there being "one true love" for each of us; and that when we are "chosen" by our lovers, we are so because we are special.

Sexual exclusivity is also important to monogamy. Sexual exclusivity requires that relata refrain from having sex with other people for as long as the romantic relationship lasts. Sexual activities are reserved for the dyadic couple. The reasons for this requirement also vary. Some reasons reflect the desire for speciality mentioned above. Other reasons center around nuclear family planning or sexual health.[25] The thought is that restricting the number of sexual partners to one at a time not only mitigates the risk of contracting sexually transmitted infections but also offers the possibility of forming a nuclear family structure with one's relata.

Both the emotional and sexual exclusivity components of monogamy are admittedly a bit obscure. As already mentioned, monogamy is sometimes cast against some forms of non-monogamy such as infidelity or cheating. That some people cheat is enough to make a perspicuous mind curious about the monogamous imaginary. I've said that the monogamous imaginary is characterized by the belief that romantic relationships *are* emotionally and sexually exclusive. When these conditions are violated, we might reasonably ask whether monogamy is characterized more by the *belief* that romantic relationships are emotionally or sexually exclusive.

One might suggest instead that it is *the desire* for emotional or sexual exclusivity that characterizes the monogamous imaginary. Yet, this is not very clever. A straightforward response is that when the integrity of so-called monogamous relationships is compromised by infidelity, they are no longer monogamous; they are non-monogamous. More interesting conversations would involve discussing whether the newly non-monogamous relationship is an ethical one all things considered.

Monogamy's exclusivities are further complicated by the consideration that sometimes lovers in dyadic monogamous relationships permissibly have sex with others such as swingers or in "threesomes". In recent years, scholars have attributed the term "monogamish"—a colloquialism to refer to relationships that are monogamous in name but also allow for agreed-upon outside sexual relationships—to media personality Dan Savage. While "swinging" involves having sex outside of the dyadic relationship, the focus tends to be physical and not emotional or intimate—monogamish. In these cases, dyadic partners negotiate allowances for inviting others into their shared sexual space usually without calling into question whether their relationship is "monogamous". The sense that we might understand these relationships as monogamous instead of monogamish is indeed obscure. However, there is a rationale where we might legibly understand these relationships as monogamies even if they are not straightforwardly so in the strictest sense.

WHAT IS NON-MONOGAMY?

For some, "Monogamy as a term, concept, and practice always and already defines the other romantic and sexual intimacies measured in relation to it and vice versa."[26] As the predominant ideology, conventional monogamy extends its power of definition over romantic and sexual intimacies.

Throughout this book, I take non-monogamy to be a *privative* concept—the rejection or negation of an idea—emerging from monogamy. Philosopher Zach Biondi makes this point.[27] On Biondi's view, non-monogamy is a privation and "does not necessarily offer any positive content of its own. This is why there are so many varieties of open relationships."[28] In my view, non-monogamy is the rejection of monogamy's core beliefs that romantic relationships are dyadic and romantically exclusive.[29]

As kinds of intimacies, monogamy and non-monogamy need one another. Some have argued that monogamy relies on the vilification of non-monogamy for its purported virtue. The point I care to make here is a conceptual one and needn't make any judgments about monogamies or non-monogamies.

In other words, there is no "non-monogamy" without "monogamy".

I take this conceptual point to be rather rudimentary and uncontroversial. While the conceptual point can be made without an evaluation, it is important to note that the legacy non-monogamies carry with them is wretched. Historically, in both the United States and Canada, non-monogamies have been treated and regarded as threats to their respective nations since the late 1800s.[30] Non-monogamies were said to be threats not only to the nation's capitalistic economies but also to Christianity and white supremacy.[31]

Additionally, polygamy—the practice or condition of having more than one *spouse* at a time—has not historically won much favor among many feminist critics. Furthermore, surveying research on non-monogamies reveals a dispro-portionate focus on polygamy often as an exemplar for thinking about non-monogamies, showing their conflation to be common. On some views, polygamy is structurally inept and rife with oppressive consequences among differ-ently gendered spouses. As such, on these views "polygamy, as traditionally conceived is morally objectionable because it precludes genuine equality between spouses."[32] Gregg Strauss writes that most polygamist communities discriminate based on gender and sexuality by permitting only polygyny.[33] Men may marry multiple women, but women may not marry multiple men, and no one may marry someone of the same sex.[34] Other views criticize polygamy based on studies that report lower quality of life for polygamous women, despite other studies that highlight enhanced agency among polyg-amous women.[35]

On its face, polygamy rejects both dyadism and monog-amous exclusivities. Importantly, a rejection of monogamy needn't make direct reference to marriage; let alone a reference to marriage at all. While polygamy is rightly characterized as non-monogamy, it is not the only shape that non-monogamy may take on. Non-monogamy scholars often mention that non-monogamies take on many forms including adultery, cheating, being intentionally single, swingers, polygamy (whether polygynous or polyandrous), polyfidelity, polyamory, open marriages and relationships, friendships, friends with benefits, group-sex such as threesomes, and other non-monogamies that are beyond the scope of those mentioned here.

The non/monogamous spectrum enables us to disambiguate varying forms of non-monogamy along different points of the spectrum. For example, while adultery and polyamory are themselves both kinds of non-monogamies, they are different in how they take shape and are governed by differing beliefs regarding non-monogamy.

Focusing a bit on these non-monogamies will help bring into finer relief the distinction between non-monogamy as an ideology and its instantiations in the world. Non-monogamy thus functions as a broader umbrella term for a collection of various relationship types, all of which reject monogamy's dyadism and exclusivities. Before shifting our focus to various kinds of non-monogamies, we'd do well to develop an understanding of the non/monogamous spectrum.

THE *NON/MONOGAMOUS* SPECTRUM

In *Fraught Intimacies: Non/Monogamy in the Public Sphere* (and elsewhere throughout his oeuvre on non-monogamy), Nathan Rambukkana is skeptical of the mutual distinctiveness of monogamy and non-monogamy. He holds that our intimate relationships are mediated by socio-political and socio-cultural spaces. Intimate relationships are not merely subject to socio-political and socio-cultural spaces, they also create them. According to Rambukkana, "Intimacies create spaces: social, national, cultural, subcultural, familial, sexual; such spaces define and constrain what forms of relationship are seen as legible, viable, ethical, legal, even real."[36] What motivates him is the search for a single system for identifying which intimate relationships are more or less privileged than others. He writes that monogamy and non-monogamy "are two sides of the same socio-cultural coin."[37] He continues, "what we think of in isolation as 'monogamy' is merely one surface of a more complex non/monogamous system that structures much of how we, configure and even strive to refigure intimate relationships."[38] He calls this system non/monogamy. Thus, I too will be using the language of non/monogamy to describe the situation between monogamies and non-monogamies. I should also make clear, then, that when I use the term 'non-monogamy', I am referring to an instantiation of some kind of non-monogamous way of relating within the non/monogamous spectrum.

For Rambukkana, "Monogamy and non-monogamy are less binary opposites, an opposed pair whose sides play off each other, than they are two aspects of a single system for relating sexually, romantically, socially, and culturally, with multiple parts and different articulations."[39] Monogamous and non-monogamous relationships are a part of the same discourse—they are intimate relationships, albeit ones that reflect different beliefs. Some others have recognized this as well. Pepper Mint writes of the relationship between monogamy and its non-monogamous adversary, cheating, and says:

monogamy needs cheating in a fundamental way. In addition to serving as the demonized opposite of monogamy, the mark of the cheater is used as a threat to push individuals to conform to monogamous behavior and monogamous appearances.[40]

Mimi Schippers echoes Mint in saying that narratives about adultery and cheating are important mechanisms for propping monogamy up as an unscathed hegemonic norm. Schippers says that in cheating narratives, socially, cheaters are "collectively punished, [and] others are discouraged from engaging in the [non-monogamous] behavior."[41] Instead of casting monogamy and non-monogamy as opposed to one another, these authors see them as having a necessary interplay. Importantly, this interplay reveals "a variegated and interpenetrating field of relationships, hardly a binary at all outside of the highly limited heteronormative mould that casts them as separate."[42]

The concept of non/monogamy is useful because being a kind of intimacy is a thread that runs through monogamies and non-monogamies alike. Of course, in addition to romantic relationships, kinships, and friendships, the scope of intimate relationships may include other "kinds of connection that [have an] impact on people, and on which they depend for a living," according to Lauren Berlant.[43] Relationships that are more traditionally thought of as not at all intimate, such as that between citizens or co-workers, are also reformed under this view. They become intimate relationships although they vary in degree.

Complete with this understanding of the non/monogamy spectrum, I now turn our attention to mapping the margins of non/monogamy.

Mapping the Margins of Non/Monogamy: Some Non-Monogamies

I do not have the space to cover every single non-monogamy that might emerge under the non-monogamous umbrella. However, some forms are worth mentioning because they sketch the terrain of the non/monogamy spectrum. They help us carve out space to make claims about moral permissibility and privilege. In this section, I discuss cheating, polyamory & polyfidelity, friendships, and singles. While this list is not complete, important features of these non-monogamies will shape our landscape.

Cheating/Adultery

Although non-monogamy takes on many forms, for many readers cheating or adultery is the most readily recognizable form of non-monogamy. As I understand it, non-monogamy is a privative concept and offers no positive content of its own. So, the assumption that non-monogamy is about a romantic or sexual relationship, is misguided.

Default assumptions made about monogamy enable disapproving attitudes about cheating and adultery. For example, regarding non-monogamous women as "ho's", "sluts", or "home-wreckers", or non-monogamous men as "players" or "cheaters", can be traced back to monogamous ideology. Monogamy is a fulcrum point from where negative attitudes and judgments about non-monogamy extend. According to Schippers, the narratives that are affixed to "cheaters" perpetuate hegemonic power as those who deviate from monogamy "are collectively and publicly punished, [and] others are discouraged from engaging in the behavior."[44] Rambukkana also sees the relationship between adultery and monogamy saying, "Adultery [keeps] the couple socially intact through subterfuge".[45] This subterfuge includes using cheaters and adulterers as props against which "normal [lovers] can measure their morals."[46] Thus, monogamy and cheating have a relationship that is on tenterhooks in amatonormative and mononormative societies.

The demonization of cheating and adultery does not end with monogamists. In contemporary discussions of non-monogamy, there is a common distinction made between "ethical non-monogamy" and other non-monogamies that, in some way or other, fall short of this moral achievement. The distinction is often made by alluding to the values that non-monogamists hold in high esteem. Ethical non-monogamists value honesty, communication, and non-possessiveness (to name a few). Thus, many of them take their practices to differ from other kinds of non-monogamy that disregard these values (e.g., cheaters who are dishonest).

Cheating and adultery are not always demonized. Sometimes they are privileged, valorized, and rewarded. In some places, adultery and cheating have been linked to what one writer calls "heteronormative capitalist individualism."[47] He points at the commodification and commercialization of adultery and claims that the adultery industry occupies a large sector of the dating industry. Particularly, Rambukkana questions the intersection of adultery and capitalism. According to Christian Klesse, websites like AshleyMaddison.com are adultery-oriented and "markets adultery with a mixture of pseudo-feminist discourse of gender equality and evolutionist psychology."[48] Attracting those with whom their slogan, "When Monogamy Becomes Monotony" resonates, the site "is the most prominent online dating service devoted to adultery."[49] Rambukkana maintains that "Feminist and sex-positive arguments are mobilized by this site but solely in the service of a commodified pro-adultery discourse, distorting important messages to make them fit in the agency's neoliberal model of adultery-as-business."[50] AshleyMaddison.com and other services like it, reveal that adultery and cheating are not only socially legible but also normalized in a way that makes their exploitation of capital possible. So even though these non-monogamies are the object of deplorability, disrespect, and contempt, they are "recognized as a part of "normal" (i.e., heteronormative) sexuality; this allows [them] a certain privilege in the public sphere."[51]

Despite much moral censure, the legibility of these non-monogamies relies very much on the legibility of monogamy as a default socio-cultural organizing principle for intimate relationships. Bearing this connection to monogamy, cheating and adultery offer what Rambukkana calls "subaltern logics" that function to uphold monogamy's value and its subsequent privileges. The legibility of cheating and adultery usher in its eligibility for privilege and reward (although it is tethered to monogamy in ways that do not allow them to mobilize power or capital in the same ways as their monogamous counterparts). This is why, for example, AshleyMaddison.com's slogan combines the often-routine monotony of some monogamies with a rationale for justifying a kind of non-monogamy. Being marketed as an alternative to monogamy, adultery can be commercialized and commodified in ways that some other non-monogamies are not (e.g., friendship, singledom, polyamory, etc.). This reveals more about the *non/monogamy* spectrum and adultery's station in it. The juxtaposition between these non-monogamies and monogamies brings a unifying thread to light—that despite their differences, each relationship indexes intimacy. This is all that the non/monogamy spectrum requires.

Non/monogamy shows cheating and adultery to be rather complex non-monogamies. It also shows that intimate privilege is never absolute so long as comparisons of various non-monogamies (and monogamies) will always find other intimate relationships (e.g., friendships, co-nationals, etc.) as their comparative counterparts. So, while cheating and adultery are in many ways subjugated to monogamy in amatonormative societies in certain respects, they are perversely privileged when compared to other intimacies.

Polyamory and Polyfidelity

At another point along the non/monogamy spectrum, we should expect to find polyamory, polyfidelity, and other forms of what are colloquially called "open relationships."[52] As research in the philosophy of love has been growing around non-monogamies, polyamory has gotten more attention in scholarship and has grown in importance around thinking about non-monogamies. In different places, writers have discussed polyamory as "a form of non-monogamy grounded in the belief in people's capacity to share and multiply their love in honest and consensual ways"[53]; "a type of consensual non-monogamy in which individuals are in or are open to multiple loving, romantic, and/or sexual relationships with the knowledge and consent of everyone involved"[54]; "A form of association in which people openly maintain multiple romantic, sexual and/or affective relationships"[55]; and "the assumption that it is possible, valid, and worthwhile to maintain intimate, sexual and/or loving relationships with more than one person [at a time]."[56]

Sheff and Hammer note that "Neither academicians nor community members have achieved consensus on precise definitions of … polyamory."[57] For our purposes, I understand polyamory as the participation in more than one romantic relationship at a time with the knowledge and consent of all of the parties involved. A satisfactory view of polyamory should capture a wide range of relationships. While some romantic relationships are sexual, others are not. Some romantic relationships are emotionally close and others are not. It should be noted that polyamory presupposes the validity of multiple and simultaneous romantic relationships whether or not they are (or ever become) sexually or emotionally (more) intimate.

In social discourse, people make distinctions between polyamory and other non-monogamies that share its "poly" prefix, such as polygamy. It is important to understand that polyamory differs from polygamy in some central ways. For example, while polyamory is the participation in multiple romantic relationships with the knowledge and consent of everyone involved, polygamy simply means multiple spouses. While conceptually each of these relationships are gender neutral (i.e., they make no gendered distinction as to who may have multiple partners), polyamory has no formal affiliation with marriage. Even though it is true that some polyamorists are married, a person who is polyamorous and married may technically still only have one spouse (i.e., their other relationships may be romantically, sexually, or emotionally intimate, all while stopping short of being marital). Polygamy does break down further, however. In non-monogamous discourse, polygamous relationships are sometimes referred to in their gendered forms such as polyandry (a woman with multiple husbands) or polygyny (one man having multiple wives). In polyamorous theory and praxis, on the other hand, "both men and women have access to multiple partners in polyamorous relationships, distinguishing them from those that are polygynous or polyandrous."[58]

Another place differentiation occurs between polyamory and polygamy may have to do with the degree of openness the relationships contain. Familiarization with the language of polyfidelity will help us see this point. Polyfidelity is a term that non-monogamists use to describe relationships that are "based in sexual and emotional fidelity among a group larger than a dyad."[59] While some polyamorous relationships are also polyfidelitous (i.e., polyamorous relationships where there is an expectation for emotional and sexual exclusivity among the group), they needn't be. Structurally, polygamous relationships are more akin to polyfidelitous relationships than polyamorous relationships are. A hallmark of polyfidelitous relationships is that they replace "the bilateral and asymmetrical demand of exclusivity characteristic of monogamous romantic relationships with a multilateral exclusivity."[60] This multilateral exclusivity characterizes the relationship in a way that it does not for polyamorists, generally speaking, as polyamorists tend to be more open in their commitment styles than those who practice polyfidelity.

Sheff highlights the fact that the language of "polyfidelity" has been controversial historically within non-monogamous communities.[61] In some cases, its impact has been divisively rigid and wedge-generating distinctions have been made between polyamory and polyfidelity, for example. A consequence, as Christian Klesse notes, is that discourses have been created around which of these non-monogamies "represents 'true' polyamory and which kinds of non-monogamy can legitimately carry the label [ethical] non-monogamy."[62] This division supports the thought that intimate relationships are on the same spectrum and intimate privilege is varied depending on where one's intimacies are positioned along this spectrum. It also demonstrates that the normative regimes (upon which such privilege rests) do not end with mono-, hetero-, and amatonormativity, but may extend to what Rambukkana calls *polynormativity*—a gatekeeping subculture that emerges from the community,[63], making "polyamor[ies], a fraught, inaccessible, or oppressive space for many."[64] One trouble with this subterranean form of communal governance, however, is that the emergent frameworks often reproduce normative standards that are less than fair and favor the already privileged among non-monogamists. He remarks, "poly individuals—as they are never 'just polys' but are located along multiple axes of privilege/oppression—cannot be seen collectively as an oppressed class. For some, polygamists might contribute to a situation of material oppression, for others, it might act to enhance entwined forms of privilege and for others, it might have no such effect whatsoever."[65]

There will be more space to explore power and privilege in Chapter 4. At present, suffice it to say that polyamories and polyfidelities chart another point along the spectrum of non-monogamies where the ethicality of relational practices is hotly contested and disputed. This contentious discourse is not confined to scholarship and academic researchers. In the age of social media, these discourses are unfolding concurrently among polyamorists who utilize their online platforms to spread information to folks who want to learn more about non-monogamy and polyamory. Still, I am of the mind that polyamories and polyfidelities prove to be fine examples of ethically permissible non-monogamies (among others). As such, it is these relationship styles that we will return to in the coming chapters to explain why it's ok to not be monogamous.

Friendship

Some may think that friendship is an unlikely candidate for non-monogamy. For example, we have likely heard claims of the sort, "Friendships are not the same thing as romantic relationships" or "You can't compare friendships to romantic relationships because they are just different kinds of things". But friendships and romantic relationships do have quite a bit in common. After all, each mode of relationship contains some amount of intimacy, care, and expectations of mutual support. It is also true that many romantic lovers (monogamous and non-monogamous alike) wish their partners to be more than just their romantic lovers, but that they also are one of their closest friends. This troubles the thought that friendships are not the same thing as romantic relationships.

Although I believe a compelling case can be made for thinking that romantic relationships are a kind of friendship, I will not present that argument here. What matters for our purposes is a simpler claim—namely, insofar as friendships are a kind of intimate relationship (even if they are a "different kind" of intimate relationship), they are still situated along the non/monogamy spectrum. Generally speaking, friendships are straightforwardly non-monogamous in that they are not dyadic. As Harry Chalmers has pointed out, friendships are an important human good that we generally wish for people to have over their lifetime.[66] Typically, friends do not intentionally make accessing this good more cumbersome. In other words, we would think there to be something morally (and perhaps socially) suspicious about friendships where friends prevent others from pursuing, establishing, or sustaining other friendships, all else equal. More than this, it is uncontroversial that we usually do pursue, sustain, and exist in friendships with more than just one person.

Despite their status as a human good, "friendships...are not accorded the social importance of marriage or marriage-like relationships" even though "for many people, friendships play a similar role in their lives, and have the same importance to them, as marriages or amorous relationships do for others. For some people, these friendships are explicitly seen as replacing, and preferable to, amorous relationships."[67] For this and other reasons, some have defended arguments for marriage reforms that include the extending rights and privileges of marriage to include friendship. Friendships as a kind of intimate relationship model have factored prominently in Elizabeth Brake's work on marriage reform, for example.

For Brake, amatonormativity privileges romantic love and sex relationships that are dyadic at the expense of other forms of caring relationships. It "wrongly privileges the central, dyadic, exclusive, enduring amorous relationship associated with, but not limited to, marriage."[68] The wrongness of this privilege is found in its function. Amatonormativity discriminates against friendships and other intimate relationships in favor of marriage and marriage-like relationships. In many contexts, people report that their friendships are not treated with the same social significance that romantic lovers are. Thus, the social dimension of amatonormativity partly "consists in evaluative judgments regarding such friendships and their members."[69] Yet, the evaluative judgments that amatonormativity makes are false and that is why they are morally problematic. For some, friendships or multi-party romantic relationships are just as (or even more) valuable than monogamous ones. Both Brake and Chalmers have issued challenges to identify morally relevant distinctions between friendships and romantic relationships. Recent philosophical responses have been less than compelling.[70] The truth is, that friendships are intimate relationships that are morally on a par with romantic relationships in both their function and significance.[71]

Despite this, amatonormativity functions in a way that precludes the formation of friendships. Brake maintains that "amatonormativity undermines relationships other than amorous love and marriage by relegating them to cultural invisibility or second best…[it] sustains the belief that marital and amorous relationships should be valued over friendships, and this undermines the attempt to pursue enduring friendships."[72] Because loving and longstanding friendships are not socially or politically incentivized in amatonormative societies, they become less salient options among a range of intimate relationships available to folks.

Another way that amatonormativity precludes the formation of friendships is by restricting the scope of what friendships are and can be. Brake claims that friendships lack a widely acknowledged social script to establish their significance. A careful mind should hesitate here as Caroline Simon's work problematizes this thought. To say that folks are "just friends" "conversationally implies (1) that Edna and Snyder are not 'sleeping together' and (2) that [these relationships are] of comparatively less significance because they are not sexually involved."[73] While there is no script for friendships that put them on a par with romantic relationships, it is a slight overstatement to say that there is no social script to establish the significance of friendships at all. For example, under *non/monogamy*, friendships are still generally revered and valued more highly than the relationships we have with strangers or acquaintances. Additionally, the script for platonic friendships is derived from amatonormative relationships. Juxtaposed to these relationships, platonic friends are conventionally understood as non-sexual at the least, and not at all physically intimate when this view is taken to its extreme. We are inclined to believe friends are "just friends" when their relationship(s) lack romantic feelings or sexual activity between the relata. Whatever judgments we might have about this view, it is uncontroversial to point out that the view is relatively widespread. What results is that some friendships are delegitimized such as friends-with-benefits relationships or romantic friendships.[74] Thus, amatonormativity constrains not only what romantic love relationships can be, but also what friendships can be (i.e., they are the kinds of things romantic relationships are not). So, while it is true that prizing monogamous relationships discourages the pursuit of friendships, it also constrains the conceptual space around thinking about what friendships are or what they can be.

The relationship between amatonormativity and friendship then is striking. Identifying discrimination that friends face because of amatonormativity is to position friendships as governed by *non/monogamy*. The scripts for romantic relationships and friendships are indeed different. Amatonormativity reveals the privileges reserved for and associated with marriage and monogamous romantic relationships. While they often are valuable and more privileged than the relationships that we have with mere strangers, friendships are not necessarily included in the same protected class of relationships as monogamous ones. Monogamous romantic relationships are the beneficiaries of economic, legal, and social incentives that create compulsory pressure to enter into these relationships. Brake writes that these "pressures to enter amorous love relationships likely result in individuals viewing friendships as less valuable than they might otherwise, and in some cases choosing less fulfilling relationships given their idiosyncratic needs and preferences, than they otherwise might."[75] Confronting this realization, we might reasonably ask what, if any, is the relationship between monogamy and capital of various kinds including social, political, and economic? That is, what is monogamy's relationship to capitalism? I set these questions aside for another day.

Singles

Singles are perhaps the least likely group one would expect to encounter in a section charting the contours of non-monogamy. As Ali Ziegler et al. note, "One way in which people can deviate from monogamy is by having no partners."[76] By single, I have in mind people who are uncoupled, not merely the unmarried. Socially, single people are not participating in a romantic relationship at all; let alone, more than one of them. However, the assumption that one must be in multiple romantic and/or sexual relationships fundamentally misunderstands non-monogamy. Earlier, I pointed out that non-monogamy is a privative concept; one that does not necessarily offer any positive content of its own. It is a negation of monogamy. Thus, non-monogamy does not *require* that one be in more than one sexual or romantic relationship (or any at all). Singles have the potential to disrupt *non/monogamy*, amatonormativity, and mononormativity because they challenge central assumptions about the importance of romantic love and about what we should expect from a well-lived life.

By not participating in romantic relations, singles occupy a space outside of monogamy. This space is sometimes imbued with a desire for participation in romantic or sexual relationships that converge with monogamy. This may be the case, for example, for a single person who desires a monogamous relationship or one who identifies as monogamous. As such, the extent to which any particular single person is active in disrupting non/monogamy will vary. The disruptive potential of singles, then, also exists on a spectrum and is partially determined by the reasons one has for being single.

People are single for any number of reasons. For example, sometimes the process of dating can be challenging and compatibility (especially monogamous compatibility) can be hard to come by. Additionally, "super singles" are intentionally single because they do not judge romantic or sexual relationships to be a necessary part of the well-lived life.[77] Singles are important for our purposes here because they point out the flaw in the assumption that one must be presently participating in a romantic or sexual relationship to be impacted by non/monogamy. In other words, while singles exist outside of a space of monogamy, they do not exist in a space exempting the reach of non/monogamy.

Singles are not exempt from non/monogamy's assumptions. Importantly, both mononormativity and amatonormativity are social phenomena that are buttressed by non/monogamy. Non/monogamy is a metaphysical framework for understanding intimate relationships and a tool for evaluating them. It is within its confines that mononormative and amatonormative pressures and judgments get their shape. It is also within its confines that singles are held accountable to its standards.

In a couple of places, Bella DePaulo and others have discussed the notion of "singlism" or the notion that people are judged to be inferior for belonging to the class of singles.[78] Singles are stereotyped for their non-participation in formal romantic or sexual relationships. They are seen as irresponsible, selfish, and lacking maturity.[79] Brake astutely observes how singles are portrayed in media as she writes "the single heterosexual man is stereotyped as an unkempt and irresponsible man-child waiting for marriage to make him a responsible adult, whereas the unmarried woman is stereotyped as lonely, desperately seeking love, and filling her empty life with cats."[80]

Whether one is single or coupled not only has social consequences but also political and economic consequences as well. Singles are paid less and their time away from work is less respected than their married counterparts as "singles widely report being expected to work evenings and holidays, to take on assignments involving extensive travel, and otherwise being treated by employers as if their nonwork commitments were less important than those of married co-workers."[81] The extent that marriage and romantic dyads are incentivized underscores the ways that singles are impacted by non/monogamy's pull:

> economic, legal, and social incentives exert great pressure to enter amorous love relationships, especially when other options appear less appealing and salient, as when singles are depicted as lonely rather than as surrounded by loving friends. The amatonormative assumption that

"singles" are seeking romantic love, and are incomplete without it, parallels the confining assumptions of "sexual liberation": The Focus on 'sexual liberation' has always carried with it the assumption that one 'should' be engaged in sexual activity.[82]

Many of the economic, legal, and social incentives are tethered to marriage. Married persons receive tax benefits and legal protections for example. Marriage also has adverse social consequences for women who were once married and are married no longer, for example. In other words, while unmarried persons can move in and out of monogamous (and non-monogamous) relationships without stigma and perhaps little shame, formerly married persons will always exist under the social moniker of a divorcée.

I will make one final point about singles and their relationship to both non-monogamy and non/monogamy. It is rather curious that in the U.S., "dating" or "talking" is colloquially understood as a kind of intimacy where positive non-monogamy (i.e., having multiple relationships at the same time with or without the mutual consent of the parties involved) is allowed and encouraged. This phenomenon is curious because the attitudes extended to singles who are actively non-monogamous in this way is one of acceptance and even praise; whereas their non-monogamous counterparts such as polyamorists and polyfidels are instead often stigmatized, stereotyped, and treated as social pariahs. The irony is that singles, polyamorists, and polyfidels, sometimes find themselves engaged in the same intimate practices only to receive differential treatment. Even though this section has primarily outlined the ways that singles are adversely impacted by non/monogamy, when compared to polyamorists and polyfidels, the spectrum reveals again just how some intimacies are privileged over others. Singles are undoubtedly disadvantaged in many ways, but their standing in relation to other non-monogamists highlights the fact that they are also beneficiaries of some degree of intimate privilege. So, while intimate privilege is not universal, the disadvantage for some kinds of intimacies is not absolute.

SUMMARY

Dyadic monogamy is socially and culturally embedded throughout Western culture, including the United States. However, it is not always clear that we know what is meant by monogamy. Throughout this chapter, I argued that monogamy is a social convention that centralizes dyadic relationships that are romantically exclusive—i.e., both sexually and emotion-ally exclusive. Specifically, the convention is a system of beliefs about romantic relationships, namely, that they are attitude-dependent, dyadic, and romantically exclusive.

In this chapter, I have also argued that non-monogamy is a negation of the social conventional values and beliefs that con-stitute monogamy. Specifically, I argued that non-monogamy is a privative concept that offers no positive content of its own. This positions non-monogamy as a category that is defined against the dominant way of doing relationships, ultimately filling out the other end of what Rambukkana calls the non/monogamy spectrum.

The non-monogamy end of the non/monogamy spec-trum covers a wide range of relationship types along with beliefs and values about intimate (romantic) relationships. As exemplars of kinds of intimacies that we might find on the non-monogamy end of the non/monogamy spectrum, I looked at singles, friendship, cheating/adultery, polyamory, and polyfidelity. While some of these intimacies, such as cheating and polyamory, are already ingrained in the social imaginary as kinds of non-monogamies, others such as singles and friendship take a more refined understanding of non-monogamy as a negation of monogamy to make legible.

REFERENCES

Alexander, Apryl A. "'We Don't Do That!': Consensual Non-Monogamy in HBO's Insecure." *Journal of Black Sexuality and Relationships* 6, no. 2 (2019): 1–16.

American Association for Marriage and Family Therapy. "Infidelity." Accessed December 28, 2021. www.aamft.org/Consumer_Updates/Infidelity.aspx.

Barker, Meg, and Darren Langdridge, eds. *Understanding Non-monogamies*. 23. Routledge, 2010.

Berlant, Lauren. *The Queen of America goes to Washington City*. Duke University Press, 1997.

Biondi, Zach. "Open Relationships are for Everybody." Accessed December 30, 2021. https://thevimblog.com/2018/08/26/open-relationships/

Brake, Elizabeth. *Minimizing Marriage: Marriage, morality, and the law*. Oxford University Press, 2012.

Brake, Elizabeth. "Recognizing care: The case for friendship and polyamory." *Syracuse Journal of Law and Civic Engagement (SLACE)* 1, no. 1 (2015): 441.

Butler, Judith. *Undoing Gender*. Psychology Press, 2004.

Chalmers, Harry. "Is Monogamy Morally Permissible?." *The Journal of Value Inquiry* 53, no.2 (2019): 225–241.

Chartier, Gary. "Marriage: A Normative Framework." *Florida Coastal Law Review* 9 (2007): 347.

Clardy, Justin and Alicia-Bunyan Sampson. "Disclosures Vol. 2: Unrecognizable B.U.D.D.Y's." *Medium*, Accessed December 30, 2021, https://urfavfilosopher.medium.com/?p=30c540d91969

Clardy, Justin. "Musings: Romantic Friendships." *Medium*, Accessed December 30, 2021, https://urfavfilosopher.medium.com/musings-romantic-frienships-b3ce02a4d7a7.

Clardy, Justin Leonard. "Monogamies, Non-Monogamies, and the Moral Impermissibility of Intimacy Confining Constraints." *Journal of Black Sexuality and Relationships* 6, no. 2 (2019): 17–36.

DePaulo, Bella. *Singled Out: How singles are stereotyped, stigmatized, and ignored, and still live happily ever after.* Macmillan, 2006.

Enns, Diane. *Love in the Dark: Philosophy by another name.* Columbia University Press, 2016.

Haritaworn, Jin, Chin-ju Lin, and Christian Klesse. "Poly/logue: A critical introduction to polyamory." *Sexualities* 9, no. 5 (2006): 515–529.

Hidalgo, Danielle Antoinette, Kristen Barber, and Erica Hunter. "The dyadic imaginary: Troubling the perception of love as dyadic." *Journal of Bisexuality* 7, no. 3–4 (2008): 171–189.

Jenkins, C. S. I. "Modal monogamy." *Ergo, an Open Access Journal of Philosophy*, 2 (2015).

Klesse, Christian. "Theorizing multi-partner relationships and sexualities— Recent work on non-monogamy and polyamory." *Sexualities* 21, no. 7 (2018): 1109–1124.

Klesse, Christian. *The Spectre of Promiscuity: Gay male and bisexual non-monogamies and polyamories.* Routledge, 2016.

Kolodny, Niko. "Love as valuing a relationship." *The Philosophical Review* 112, no. 2 (2003): 135–189.

McMurtry, John. "Monogamy: A critique." *The Monist* (1972): 587–599.

Mint, Pepper. "The power dynamics of cheating: Effects on polyamory and bisexuality." *Journal of Bisexuality* 4, no. 3–4 (2004): 55–76.

Pincus, Tamara, and Rebecca Hiles. *It's Called "Polyamory": Coming Out About Your Nonmonogamous Relationships.* Thorntree Press LLC, 2017.

Rambukkana, Nathan. *Fraught Intimacies: Non/monogamy in the public sphere.* UBC Press, 2015.

Rambukkana, Nathan. "Open non-monogamies." In *The Palgrave Handbook of the Psychology of Sexuality and Gender*, 236–260. London: Palgrave Macmillan, 2016.

Rambukkana, Nathan, and Wilfrid Laurier. "Protecting the Intimate Space of the Nation: Intimacy, Privilege and Canadian Antipolygamy Laws 1892–2012." Accessed December 30, 2021, https://d1wqtxt s1xzle7.cloudfront.net/32348223/Rambukkana_-_Protecting_ the_Intimate_Space_of_the_Nation__SSA13_Talk-with-cover-page- v2.pdf?Expires=1640918036&Signature=YlyPGpAib-uExsiwVfce bHTlFfnce1CCSHXwPQI5RTw-ta06mA-VkMMGwAl0RegCjfSjsiB i3Qe0sWDxAV-mdstG89Zgt0o9VAASMjllHld8fGn5XkxKhcqMH vVvxhp79jotoOLw-qujm7PnpUwWtRmLLgmhFVxgTqlmFh7Fo y3L~XAIlvgv403cfPTU2ad4DaBW8RTXP~9N1O2oug-9TEMmlEw1 zfuvYr3-2hblTGIR2AiyXk6Geu4T0uttR144uJjF1ftvrlsNoj3XrHug tcd-5XUd5NpC35JutQenuyh5eFSjy95wVAdXmalCa~uxeGd7~8o8 Mvg~BYjdXK95ow__&Key-Pair-Id=APKAJLOHF5GGSLRBV4ZA.

Ritchie, Ani, and Meg Barker. "'There aren't words for what we do or how we feel so we have to make them up': Constructing polyamorous languages in a culture of compulsory monogamy." *Sexualities* 9, no. 5 (2006): 584–601.

Schippers, Mimi. *Beyond Monogamy: Polyamory and the future of polyqueer sexualities.* Vol. 13. NYU Press, 2016.

Sheff, Elisabeth. *The Polyamorists Next Door: Inside multiple-partner relationships and families.* Rowman & Littlefield, 2015.

Sheff, Elisabeth, and Corie Hammers. "The privilege of perversities: Race, class, and education among polyamorists and kinksters." *Psychology & Sexuality* 2, no. 3 (2011): 198–223.

Simon, Caroline J. "Just Friends, Friends and Lovers, or …?" *Philosophy and Theology* 8, no. 2 (1993): 113–128.

Strauss, Gregg. "Is Polygamy Inherently Unequal?." *Ethics* 122, no. 3 (2012): 516–544.

Whitty, Monica T. "The realness of cybercheating: Men's and women's representations of unfaithful Internet relationships." *Social Science Computer Review* 23, no. 1 (2005): 57–67.

York, Kyle. "Why Monogamy is Morally Permissible: A Defense of Some Common Justifications for Monogamy." *The Journal of Value Inquiry* (2019): 1–14.

Ziegler, Ali, Terri D. Conley, Amy C. Moors, Jes L. Matsick, and Jennifer D. Rubin. "Monogamy." In *The Palgrave Handbook of the Psychology of Sexuality and Gender*, 219–235. London: Palgrave Macmillan, 2016.

Two

INTRODUCTION

In the previous chapter, we looked at what non-monogamy is. We learned that non-monogamy is the negation of monogamy, that it offers no positive content of its own, and that it covers a wide variety of relationships and beliefs. In that chapter, I hinted at polyamory as a morally exemplary kind of non-monogamy. The current chapter picks up on this hint and focuses on polyamory in making the case for why it's OK to NOT be monogamous. I start by examining some reasons for thinking that it is not OK to be polyamorous including the belief that monogamy is natural, that monogamy is divinely ordained, the argument from specialness, the argument from sexual health, and the argument from jealousy.

I argue that the common defenses of monogamy fall short of justifying monogamy in a universal way—that is, in a way that invalidates non-monogamous romantic relationships. The sections throughout this chapter explore some common justifications of monogamy's categorical restriction on having more than one romantic partner at a time.

I now turn our attention to some of the reasons for thinking that it is not OK to be polyamorous.

DOI: 10.4324/9781003375036-3

WHY IT'S NOT OK TO BE NON-MONOGAMOUS

A variety of arguments have been offered that challenge the moral standing of non-monogamy. Even where arguments have not yet been offered, some might think there is good evidence to resist regarding non-monogamy as morally permissible. Some opponents of non-monogamy posit moral reasons that have to do with divine commands handed down to us from God. Others treat polyamory as socially destructive because it disrupts the nuclear family, a disruption that for some generates harm for society at large.[1] Throughout this section, I present arguments that are, in my view, among the most prominent rejections of polyamory. I also highlight what I take to be adequate responses to these arguments already spotted in academic literature. Along the way, I develop and extend some of these insights.

Monogamy Is Natural

Scholarship on and representation of consensual non-monogamy (CNM) and polyamory has been growing in popularity and exposure. As a result, we have also grown more aware of the attitudes lay people have about CNM relationships. Léa Séguin's discussion of lay attitudes and perceptions of polyamory focuses on how people view CNM, and specifically polyamory in a negative light.[2] While some people see polyamory as valid and beneficial, others see it as unsustainable, perverse, amoral, and unappealing. Surveying the commentary around popular blog articles on polyamory, she found that "commenters often spoke of polyamory as an unnatural practice and therefore, as something that should be avoided."[3] Insisting that humans evolved to be monogamous, these attitudes imply that multi-partnered relationships are primitive or unnatural. Other varieties of what we can call *monogamist naturalism* (or biological essentialism) hold that romantic love is a biological drive. Carrie Jenkins has recently challenged Helen Fisher's view that "love is a basic biological urge that motivates us to do things that we as a species need to do to survive and thrive."[4] Jenkins elaborates on Fisher's narrative which explains human "pair-bonding" rooted in a theory about human evolution. On Fisher's view, as bipedalism complicated females' practices of carrying children on their backs and obliged them to instead carry their offspring in their arms, having male protectors became necessary for the survival of the human species. Thus, monogamy evolved as an essential component of human survival—ensuring that humans would pair-bond with one person at a time.

Other writers have suggested that jealousy is the product of successful survival strategies for humans. Séguin describes these perspectives as "portraying jealousy not only as a normal and natural response to a partner experiencing love and sex with an outside partner, but also as playing a functional role within relationships."[5] On this view, it is ok to be monogamous because monogamy is the direction that our natures point us towards—polyamory and other non-monogamies are unnatural and, on this basis, they are not okay.

Ronald Den Otter remarks on how uncommon naturalistic arguments against multi-party relationships and marriages are.[6] Appeals to nature that attempt to rule out polyamorous relationships get most of their traction among political conservatives and religious fundamentalists. I have also encountered this objection from my students while teaching love and non-monogamy at liberal arts institutions affiliated with both Jesuits and Church of Christ denominations.

While I think it is far from the most pressing concern facing polyamorists, it is worth making a few remarks addressing these concerns for interested readers before moving on to more pressing ones.

One thing that is worth noting about naturalist views is that they presuppose what conservative writers like Robert George might call a "complimentary" sexual union.[7] For George and others, complimentary sexual unions are open to the possibility of procreation. As such, they assume that the "true" or "authentic" form of romantic relationship is heterosexual. Views such as these have been routinely used in the service of rejecting the validity of same-sex relationships. But the view goes further as it also implies that heterosexual unions, where an ability or desire for procreation is absent, are also defective.

Alan Goldman criticizes "means-ends" analyses of sex that attribute a necessary external goal or purpose to sex.[8] In making his case, he also rejects views of sex that say that it is about reproduction. Goldman reminds us that while reproduction might be nature's biological purpose for sex, it certainly needn't be ours. While eating also serves a biological function, we do not eat for this purpose only. Sometimes we eat because we take genuine pleasure in eating things. The prevalence of contraception, Goldman argues, has also rendered the connection between sex and biology weak. His view also includes a broad net for sexual acts (i.e., including kissing and caressing insofar as they involve the desire for contact with another person's body and the pleasure that it produces). Taking this broader view, Goldman maintains that positing reproduction as sex's primary or only function "fails to generate a consistent ethic: homosexual and oral-genital sex is condemned while kissing or caressing, acts equally unlikely to lead in themselves to fertilization, even when properly characterized as sexual according to our definition, are not."[9] The point here is simply that the biological argument too heavily relies on procreation in the service of species preservation in evolutionary tales of monogamy. Sex acts needn't be constrained by having procreation as its primary or only goal.

Another subtle point addresses the fact that polyamorous relationships are unnatural in that they willingly seek to subvert human nature by seeking out relationships that are bound to incite jealousy. We should hesitate before extending judgment on things that seemingly subvert the evolutionary course of the human species. For example, in 2020 amidst a global pandemic over the respiratory disease, COVID-19 (and its associated variants), vaccinations were developed that were intended to alter and slow the course of the disease's spread to preserve human life. One could argue that the introduction of the vaccine first arriving on the scene in 2020 was a kind of human intervention that disrupted the evolutionary course of the disease's spread and global impact. The fact that humans sometimes act against nature in this way suggests that acting against nature is not necessarily "wrong". This point might be extended to polyamorists who are believed to be acting against human nature by having more than one romantic relationship simultaneously.

A final point is that an appeal to nature as a way of bolstering any kind of normative force is to reside uncomfortably close to a commission of the naturalistic fallacy—which generally states that if something is "natural" it must be good. Familiarity with this fallacy reveals that it is committed when a move from "is" to "ought" is made without much explanation. To describe some feature of the world and the way that it is does little to justify the claim that that is the way things ought to be. Generally, the thought is that facts do not directly lead us to value claims. This means that the burden is on proponents of *monogamist naturalism* to demonstrate why, in this case, "acting against nature" is morally impermissible when in other cases such as vaccinations or the development of commodious buildings, is not.

Divine Ordination[10]

There is another common justification of monogamy to which philosophers have paid, so far as I can tell, very little attention. This justification tethers monogamy to moral commands given by God. John McMurtry writes that "Perhaps the most celebrated justification over the years has proceeded from a belief in a Supreme Deity who secretly utters sexual and other commands to privileged human representatives."[11] Western Christianity's New Testament narrative sends a resounding message: "And I say to you: whosoever divorces his wife, … and marries another, commits adultery"[12]; "…and whoever marries a divorced woman commits adultery."[13] The message in the Bible's Old Testament is not much different: "And he shall not acquire many wives, lest his heart turn away."[14]

It's also noteworthy that in Exodus 20: 1–3, where God speaks his commandments to Moses, the first commandment imparted to Moses involves a rejection of polytheism. God speaks to Moses saying, "I am the Lord your God, who brought you out of Egypt, out of the land of slavery. You shall have no other gods before me." Historically, some ancient civilizations like Rome and Greece, as well as populations indigenous to Western Africa have been known to practice forms of polytheism. Some of these polytheistic spiritualities and religions have non-monogamous discourses embedded in them. For instance, not only did the people of Ancient Rome believe in more than one god, some of the gods of their Pantheon were also non-monogamous. For example, the Herculean myth passed down to us from Roman mythologists posit that Zeus was consistently promiscuous and Hercules was born unto Alcemene, who some regard as Zeus' mistress. Still, it is the narratives imparted on humanity by Western Christianity that remain most salient in Western society today.

The scene between God and Moses in Exodus 20 is important for those who might have sympathies with the idea that monogamy is justified by divine ordination. Verse 15 reads explicitly "You shall not commit adultery." Many interpret this to mean that monogamy's moral status comes from God. However, we should resist this view as it contains the prerequisite that one must believe in God in the first place. This implies, for example, that atheists and agnostics are *de facto* disqualified from romantic love. This is more pressing as it holds even if they find themselves in happy, healthy, and satisfying monogamous romantic relationships. This is counterintuitive—namely that one's otherwise morally permissible monogamous dating is underwritten and overruled by their failure to believe in the Christian God.

Those that believe that monogamy is justified by a command from God, thereby constituting a monogamous moral code that is divinely ordained—or who I shall hereafter refer to as *divine ordinationists*—would seem to have other problems on their hands. Socrates asks Euthyphro "Is the pious being loved by the gods because it is pious, or is it pious because it is loved by the gods?"[15] Divine ordinationists face a similar conundrum: Is monogamy morally permissible because God says it's morally permissible, or does God say that it is morally permissible because it is morally permissible? The question poses a dilemma. If one says that monogamy is morally permissible because God says it is, it seems that God's approval is arbitrary. On the other hand, if God approves of monogamy because it is morally permissible, then its moral permissibility must be independent of God's approval—there must be some quality that is independent of what God approves, and which can serve as the basis for the approval of monogamy.

If we affirm the first horn of the dilemma (that monogamy is good/morally permissible because God says that it is) it appears that God's approval of monogamy is arbitrary and unmotivated. As a result, it appears that things like adultery or non-monogamy would be good if they had God's approval. This consideration is troubling for those who argue that moral obligations are duties because God commands them. On the second horn of the dilemma, if God is restricted to commanding the moral permissibility of monogamy because of monogamy's alleged inherent goodness, it appears that God has no choice in deciding what to command. This implies the existence of a moral and epistemic code that is superior to God's commands, situating God's subservience to it as problematic to God's alleged omnipotence.

Letting go of this Euthyphro dilemma for monogamous love relationships, there is at least one more complication that I find pressing with the divine ordination view. Even if it were the case that monogamy is divinely ordained, there must be some moral duties that are not grounded in divine commands because they seemingly hold conceptually prior to or independently of divine commands—namely, that we must obey divine commands. The duty that humans presumptively have to obey God's commands is what enables God to create new obligations or to deem some kinds of love relationships morally permissible. This prior obligation weakens the purported strength of the claim that monogamy is only morally permissible because God divinely ordained it. It would be more reasonable to expect human reverence to be directed toward the source of whatever moral standard that might be. My point here is not to present every possible challenge to divine command theory, but rather only to problematize it for those who think it ostensible that monogamy's moral permissibility is established at the helm of God's commands.

Justification from Specialness

Sometimes attempts to justify moral monogamy are made by appealing to the thought that "monogamy helps one's romantic relationships to be special."[16] On this view, the exclusivity promised by monogamy makes one's romantic relationship more special. Yet, if having only one partner makes for a more special romantic relationship, and if the value of this specialness is sufficient to justify monogamous restrictions, it is hard to see how having only one friend would not also make a friendship more special.[17] Even in the case that the quality of one's romantic relationships with multiple people may lessen if one has too many, this is hardly a restriction on having *more than one*. Instead, it foregrounds agential responsibility to identify or establish one's relational bandwidth—or an upper threshold on the kinds (or amount) of relationships one can pour into before they become what some non-monogamists call "polysaturated" (a term used by polyamorists to signal to others that they are closed off to the possibility of taking on additional relationships because the number of existing partners, or time constraints, make starting new relationships difficult).

Perhaps it is, as York nudges, that "the distinctive feeling of being the one person one's partner has chosen...might simply have to do with the fact that a relationship we make exclusive for practical reasons should be sufficiently fulfilling and significant to protect in such a way."[18] For these lovers "it is not that exclusivity makes the relationship special; it's that the specialness of the relationship justifies making it exclusive."[19] This appeal to specialness also comes up short when it comes to justifying monogamy. For instance, some non-monogamists, such as polyfidels, may also satisfy this criterion. It is true that "a relationship we make exclusive for practical reasons" could well be one with more than two relata and can be found to be sufficiently fulfilling and significant enough to think of as worthy of our protection by setting practical boundaries related to exclusivity. The notion of exclusivity, in this case, is a pluralistic one that resists mononormative and amatonormative assumptions that exclusivity implies dyadism—one that extends to non-monogamous relationships of more than two people. We could also think about how this functions in the context of exclusive social clubs such as golf clubs, fraternities, or sororities. In these contexts, members are offered exclusive benefits and privileges that non-members are not. These perks contribute to feelings of speciality even though that membership is multiplicitous.

Another threat related to specialness is the idea that non-monogamous relationships have us confront ourselves in a way that causes us to believe that there's something wrong with us and the relationship—that we are not very special at all or, worse, that we are "not enough" for our partner. The lover, then, is not as special as he takes himself to be. Monogamy functions as a kind of protection mechanism that keeps one from feeling this way. However, we must critically confront the possibility that these feelings of self-insufficiency might be bred by the common assumption that one's partner is supposed to fulfill all of our personal needs. Under this framework, "Naturally, facing such a high standard only makes it easier to feel insecure, to worry whether you're really enough for your partner."[20] But this assumption is unreasonable and based on false pretenses.

Generally, we expect partners (even in the most loving of romantic relationships) to have some (dare I say, many) of their personal needs met outside of their romantic relationship by friends, family members, children, and hobbies, for example. Building one's self-confidence independent of one's romantic relationship is one way to foster resistance against these thoughts of insufficiency. Indeed, this kind of self-surety ought to be revered in any romantic relationship. There also seems to be a workable alternative that meets the idea of self-insufficiency head-on. Instead of resisting the thinking that we are not enough for our romantic partners, we could lean into its acceptance. A perspectival shift in this fashion enables us to arrive at a more perspicuous picture of romantic love and relationships. The fact that we, generally speaking, are not enough for the satisfaction of all of our partner's needs entails little about ourselves as people. That is, one's shortcomings *qua partner* needn't be looked at as shortcomings *qua person*. Monogamy does not protect against feelings of self-insufficiency, it perpetuates them.

It is rather curious that thinking of oneself as insufficient is not as common of an occurrence in friendships when our friends take interest in having (or already have) other friends. Chalmers analogizes the following:

Once more, we might consider an analogy with friendship. To make a new friend is no indication at all that there is something wrong with an existing friend. It doesn't even remotely suggest that the existing friend "isn't enough." (And let's imagine now that the existing friend did confront us with such a charge. "What's wrong—am I not enough for you?" he demands. How sadly neurotic, how appallingly petty and immature this would be!) After all, at least in typical, healthy, cases we form friendships not to correct for some deficiency, but to add a source of value to our lives and to the lives of our friends.[21]

Chalmers' analogy reveals something important; it appropriately targets the concern as being an initial assumption that friendship-having is not deficiency-correcting. That is, in typical cases, we pursue friendships to add something to our lives and not to correct for some insufficiency in ourselves in the first place. So, too, with romantic relationships. Under contemporary Western paradigms, we do not get into relationships to correct deficiencies in ourselves; being a good partner is not like filling an empty void as Aristophanes suggests in the *Symposium*.[22] This move toward a realization that we are not our partner's everything and that not being our partner's everything needn't entail anything about insufficiency suggests that perhaps a perspectival shift is not too far afield.

Sexual Health

Some endeavor to defend moral monogamy based on sexual health. They believe that "The idea is that having multiple sexual relationships at a time leads to a much higher

risk of sexually transmitted infections (STIs) and, in heterosexual relationships of unwanted pregnancy. If partners
want to reduce risks, they are well advised to restrict sexual
relationships to one sexual relationship at a time."[23] One
might appropriately respond by pointing to the various forms
and methods of contraception and safer sex. Those who have
multiple sex partners simultaneously can drastically reduce
unwanted pregnancies and the risk of STIs through the
proper use of condoms, dental dams, IUDs, and other various
methods of risk reduction. While using these methods does
not eliminate the risk, we should critically question why such
elimination is required for love and not other risky activities
that we find meaningful, enjoyable, and even valuable.

Assume with me for the moment that Mal is a thrill seeker
whose lifestyle regularly involves practicing parkour, bungee
jumping, and white-water rafting. Imagine further that Mal
is enthralled by an opportunity that has presented itself for
them to go skydiving with a friend. It's uncontroversial that
skydiving involves the particular risks of bodily harm and
even death (which is outlined in the waiver they are required
to sign before going for their jump). It seems foolhardy to
suggest that on this basis Mal ought not to engage in such
activities or that he should prevent others from engaging in
them. Less dramatically, driving a car also contains the same
risks at a higher rate than skydiving; lest we do not think
that people ought to be restricted from the activity merely on
this basis. There seems to be no reason for thinking that non-
monogamous sex is any different.

We should also call to mind the assumption that romantic
love relationships involve sex. While this might be true
for many romantic relationships, it is far from a universal
occurrence or necessity. For example, some monogamous

or non-monogamous romantic relationships might not be sexual, as is the case for some asexual lovers. This foregrounds the fact that it is not a relationship's structure that prevents these sexual risks, but rather the relata themselves. Just as a non-sexual non-monogamous romantic relationship is possible, it is also possible that parties to a monogamous relationship might also violate monogamy by having extrarelational sex with someone(s) who is not their partner, as in the case of cheating, adultery, or group sex with their monogamous partner. This, of course, highlights the fact that monogamous restrictions do surprisingly little to prevent or preempt sexual risk.

While the above considerations address the possibility of simultaneous sexual partners, it is also not the case that monogamy alone reduces the risks involved with sexual health. We might expect this risk to be mitigated by undergoing regular testing for STIs. It is noteworthy that a good amount of literature on non-monogamy emphasizes that non-monogamists are more likely to be tested regularly for STIs than their monogamous counterparts. But the point here is to cast doubt on monogamy mitigating this risk. Although serial monogamists may exist in one and only one romantic relationship at a time, it is clear that serial monogamists have multiple partners and, perhaps, multiple loves over time. In case a serial monogamist moves from sexual monogamous relationships to other sexual monogamous relationships without being tested regularly for STIs and, say, refuses to discuss their sexual history, monogamy once again appears unsatisfactory for the mitigation of risk around sexual health.

As monogamy falls short of offering protection against the mitigation of sexual risks, risk assessments ought generally to be done case by case, with open discussion between partners whether a relationship is monogamous or non-monogamous in form. There may be genuine cases where sex with another person may not be worth the associated benefits precisely because the risk factor is too great or interest in sex with that person is low (as in the case of some asexuals). There are two primary takeaways here: (1) embracing romantic love relationships does not mean that one must be open to any sexual contact with one's romantic partner at all and (2) in the case that relating romantically does include sexual contact, all relata seeking to eliminate risks to their sexual health should do so through regular testing, contraception, and protection where access to those resources are available.

Jealousy

Of the defenses for monogamy's justification, the appeal to jealousy is perhaps the most common in literature on non-monogamy, as well as in everyday conversation about non-monogamy. Admittedly, it is not always clear what the appeal is supposed to amount to, nor why it should be taken very seriously. Jealousy is felt across a wide range of contexts, not just in our romantic relationships. This makes an appeal to the presence of jealousy as a justification for monogamy, rather curious. Be that as it may, in this section I present my understanding of the role of jealousy in doing just that. My exploration of jealousy's role in (non-)monogamous intimacies also provisionally creates space for exploring the very real, but under-discussed emotion of compersion—or the emotion that focuses on the flourishing of someone one cares about as a result of that person's interaction with other people.[24]

There can be high stakes when we date romantically. Existing in closer intimate proximity with others risks our comfort, our happiness, and (at times) our sanity. Thus, when we think about our partner taking interest in someone else, we are likely to experience anxiety, agony, despair, and self-loathing. Some believe the fear of losing our partner to someone else is at the heart of jealousy.[25] According to Chalmers, "what most often underlies our feelings is the worst that our partner will come to desire her not in *addition to* us, but *instead* of us."[26] To be sure, it is not merely the thought of our partner taking interest in someone else that triggers jealousy. Contemporary philosophers, like Luke Brunning, have pointed out that vulnerability, possessiveness, and entitlement also underpin jealousy. I am inclined to believe that beliefs tethered to entitlement do underlie jealousy. Like some others, I take jealousy to be a painful emotion that emerges from the "perceived threat from a[n] [outside] party to the attention of someone one cares about and to which one feels entitled."[27] Admitting jealousy's painfulness, lovers might be led to think that "Only monogamy can keep us safe from jealousy; that is its justification."[28]

Jealousy has come under epistemic and moral suspicion, leaving philosophers to question the logic of jealousy along with its moral standing and functionality. For example, in a reply to a claim made by Chalmers that "we feel jealous[y] precisely because we are less rational and less mature than we would be," York writes from an apologetic position and argues that jealousy is not irrational or unreasonable.[29] For the sake of precision, York is not defending universal monogamous restrictions by appealing to jealousy, instead, it is that for "*some* couples, restrictions on outside relationships help avoid risks of breaking up."[30] He continues, "Just as it's unfair to expect the same of everyone's ability to deal with snakes or heights, it's unfair to expect everyone to be able to handle jealousy in the same way. Thus, it doesn't even matter what is generally true of humans' ability to handle jealousy; if there is one couple who cannot overcome their jealousy, monogamy could be justified in their case."[31]

A couple of things should be said here. First, while jealousy may generate reasons for some couples to prohibit outside relationships to avoid the risk of breaking-up, that does not get around the consideration of whether the kind of restrictions placed on these relationships to achieve these ends passes our evaluative tests. That is, we must ask whether *any* such restriction might do. For example, insurance that one will remain the object of their lover's captivation can be achieved through solitary confinement—one could lock one's partner in a room to avoid risks of breaking up. But the achievement of the end in this way is surely morally deplorable to any lover with a healthy moral conscious. So clearly not just any restriction will do. The question is about whether the monogamous restriction is a *good* one or one that imposes undue and unallowable moral costs on the relata.

Next, because relational ideals extend beyond the personal level to social and political levels, as in the case of amatonormativity and mononormativity, York's view is also unsatisfactory in that it seemingly ignores monogamy's social and political positionality in societies that are compulsorily monogamous, mononormative, and amatonormative. "In societies where monogamy is normative, jealousy is an expected, normalized, and even praised emotion," Brunning writes.[32] The impositions placed on members of a liberal society by these logics should be enough to warrant their criticism and deconstruction. In mononormative societies "Most people are deeply committed to monogamy as a structure of romantic life, and monogamous culture makes little provision for members of couples to flourish intimately with other people."[33] It is "[a]gainst this backdrop of monogamous norms...and philosophical argument, jealousy can seem like a solid feature of romantic life; something to be managed, not removed. When jealousy looks secure and even reasonable, compersion looks fragile and even outrageous."[34]

For some defenders of jealousy, jealousy has intrinsic value. Proponents of this view might think that jealousy is somehow a part of love. The thought is that: "Like clouds heralding rain, jealousy [is] a sign that people care about their beloved. This sign is purportedly useful for the beloved as they know their affection is cherished, but also for the jealous person, as their emotions help them realize how much they care about the beloved."[35] For others, jealousy's value is instrumental—it is valued as an erotic catalyst or for preventing people from becoming indifferent to one another, or because it promotes reflection. Brunning notes that "Certain kinds of erotic context and framing narrative allow people to toy with jealousy, invoke it in others, and find it arousing... [and it] is also central to some manifestations of the cuckold fetish and in other fantasies of humiliation or displacement."[36]

Compersion

I question whether jealousy has the intrinsic value that it is purported to have. After all, even if jealousy is valuable, given that it can be painful or harmful (or indeed any other negative outcome that may be associated with jealousy), we might do better to ask whether other emotions can achieve these same ends. Compersion is an emotion that is heavily discussed among non-monogamists and focuses on how one's partner *fares* in their other intimate relationships. Some have argued that compersion offers the purported benefits of jealousy. While primarily discussed among non-monogamists, these benefits are not restricted to these relationships.

As far as combating jealousy, Brunning suggests that this emotion can be cultivated (i) by confronting and managing our vulnerability, (ii) by softening our propensity to be jealous, and (iii) by learning to pay attention to the flourishing of others. Essentially, relata must consider their expectations and boundaries.[37] One must ask:

> What do they want from a romantic relationship, and why do they want that? Are they beholden to social archetypes or personal quirks? Are they too dependent on the other? What triggers their insecurity, and how can that be managed? What affirmation do they want from a partner?… They may [also] slowly expose themselves to situations where jealousy looms to foster resilience and practice good communication; they might talk honestly about their new romantic life to make it seem less threatening because jealousy, like fear, thrives on uncertainty; they can notice how they are gripped by particular thought patterns—'what if she never comes back'—and lather their focus by seeking reassurance, and they can strive to maintain a nurturing home and community by talking to friends, make time for regular conversation, rethink how they organize their personal space, and practice rituals of affirmation and love. These practices are discussed frequently in self-help books for non-monogamous people, and draw upon cognitive behavioral therapy and other forms of emotion regulation.[38]

Importantly, these strategies require confronting jealousy straight away. Some non-monogamists, and specifically polyamorists, see the occurrence of jealousy as an opportunity for self-improvement. Polyamorists accept a narrative around love and intimate relationships that deviates from the standard social script. Acceptance of a narrative that makes it possible to have multiple loving relationships simultaneously alters the evaluative aspects of their emotional responses to their lover's flourishing with other people. Brunning writes,

> Rather than running away from their jealous feelings, as it were, by restricting their behavior so as not to trigger them, the partners should confront their jealous feelings head-on. They should take responsibility for their feelings, seek to overcome their insecurities, work to free themselves from the fears and false assumptions that give rise to the problem in the first place.[39]

To put the point plainly, it is important to interrogate the source(s) of jealousy and ask ourselves why we feel jealous when our partners express interest in other people, and more keenly, why do we not feel this way when our partners find joy in other relationships such as their friendships? Compersive emotions suggest instead, that it could make sense to be cooperative with our partners when they take on other romantic relationship interests. As Chalmers asks, "[w]ould it not be truer to love, truer to our good will, to share in [our partner's] joy?"[40]

One might argue that people should only cultivate emotional dispositions they can cultivate, that compersion is psychologically implausible, and therefore that compersion ought not be cultivated.[41] Here I submit that whether or not compersion should be cultivated depends slightly on the context of the agent in question and the relationship they are in; this is a variety of the *ought implies can* problem. For example, Jessica Fern advances an attachment theory where people's adult relationships are shaped by the pattern of attachment developed from their infancy.[42] For relata coming from severely traumatic relational pasts, the ability to foster and sustain securely attached relationships free of jealousy is a genuine problem; their traumatic pasts, it may be thought, forecloses their ability to take the suggested steps for fostering compersive emotions. For these lovers, it may be that monogamy is justifiable because it protects their bonds with their partners by meeting their unique, trauma-based needs. Ruling out monogamy's justification in cases like these may seem to uphold an ableist view of love.

Yet, while Fern's work suggests that unique challenges emerge for lovers with severely traumatic pasts, she urges that these challenges are not entirely insurmountable. So, while it might be more difficult for relata who have severely traumatic pasts, these lovers should still be encouraged to do the work of overcoming their propensity for experiencing jealousy. Lovers should not be encouraged toward this end merely because their relationship requires it, but instead because jealousy is an emotion that individuals are better off not experiencing in any context. Brunning urges, "[a]s with any emotional work, like trying to be less angry, someone can progress toward becoming compersive while still experiencing episodic lapses into jealousy."[43] So while jealousy is a barrier to experiencing compersive emotions, we have reason to take effective steps to cultivate it.

Ultimately, monogamy does not preclude jealousy. Even monogamists experience jealousy. Furthermore, there is no clear connection between jealousy and flourishing relationships.

The TEA Objection

Harry Frankfurt points out that "living without goals or purposes is living with nothing to do."[44] As idealistic as we sometimes make it out to be, love is inescapably a practical matter. Love and loving have close ties with arranging our lives purposefully and with meaning. In many respects loving others and being loved by others helps to make our activity purposeful. In other respects, love is not only a worthwhile end in itself, it also can be (and often is) a primary contributor to the establishing of ends in our lives—helping us to arrange our aims and our lives accordingly.

The practical features of love are not lost on supporters of moral monogamy. Practicality defenses of moral monogamy appeal to our limited resources such as time, energy, and attention. For example, we do not have an infinite amount of time, energy, and attention available for our partner(s) (or anything else for that matter). As a result, one "good that monogamy offers is extra time and attention available for one's partner."[45] Others have pointed to different practical considerations such as a desire for proximity to one's partner, or for cohabitation. York writes, "[i]n a committed relationship ... partners often end up moving for each other, and it's important for many couples that they would be able to do so if the necessity arose. Emotionally significant relationships with outside partner's greatly complicate this ability."[46] Notice here that York's appeal to emotional significance articulates a slightly different version of the argument. That is, "not merely time and energy management, but considerations of people's emotional limitations can justify monogamy."[47]

Chalmers responds that "The mere fact that we are incapable of devoting our romantic attention to unlimited partners at a time, hardly justifies setting the limit to *one*."[48] We should also note here that having "extra" time and attention does not necessitate that partners will be able to spend it together if their availability does not overlap; this is the case whether the relationship is monogamous or non-monogamous. Further, one might deliberately choose to spend their "extra time" *away* from their partner with a hobby or with friends in order to preserve their romantic relationship. Jessica Fern's work on secure polyamorous attachments reveals that all lovers have unique attachment styles and sometimes spending time away from one's partner is a necessary component of healthily attached relationships.[49] These concerns are practical themselves, and must be overcome by monogamists and non-monogamists alike. But these attempts justify moral monogamy—the appeal to limited time/energy/attention (hereafter the 'TEA' defense) and the appeal to emotional limitations—come up short in other ways as well.

The TEA defense can be resisted on various grounds. First, there is what I will call *the threshold problem*. That is, appealing to an inability to devote our limited time, energy, and attention to our romantic partners seems to be bound up with the idea that there is some threshold of how much TEA we must pour into a relationship in order for it to count as romantic love. This way of essentializing the conditions for romantic love constrains the agency of the parties to the relationship by prohibiting their ability to establish for themselves how much TEA they might need or want. While it is true that some partners end up moving for each other, it is a mistake to superimpose this desire for proximity or cohabitation universally to all lovers. The simple appeal to partners moving for each other also masks very real gendered and class-based asymmetries (especially in heteronormative relationships) involving which of the dyadic partners moves for the other. As a result, the appeal itself is an extension of patriarchal heteronormative, amatonormative, and mononormative pressure that (more often than not), functions to oppress and exploit women. It is also a mistake to regard non-proximate relationships as less "serious" than ones that are not, as York seems to do.

Imagine with me for the moment that Mal, Zed, and Ashley are guests at a high tea. Each of them, while all tea drinkers, have unique preferences about how much tea they take in any one cup of tea. Mal prefers his cup only one-fourth of the way full; Zed prefers their cup half full; and Ashley prefers the faux pas practice of having her cup filled to the brim (she's such a rebel). Let's also assume that proper tea etiquette prescribes that hosts pour the cup three-fourths full. Following what the convention prescribes will leave each of the guests dissatisfied with their cup of tea. One way to avoid their disappointment is to ask how much tea they take in their cup prior to pouring it.[50] Furthermore, it would seem that their preferences do not make them any less of tea drinkers.

The TEA defense of monogamy assumes that there is a requisite amount of TEA everyone's cup must have in order for their love to be legitimate. Desires for one's romantic relationship, however, are just as diverse as the preferences of our tea drinkers in the example above. Not all lovers want to live together or near each other, for example. Altering the convention by asking how much tea each guest desires to have poured has the benefit of not assuming a universal threshold around how much TEA a proper cup makes. Opponents might respond that guests at a high tea usually observe the convention's norms and as a result, they know what they are getting themselves into. After all, not all people attend high teas and the ones that do, do so based on their willing observation of the conventional norms. So too, they might say, with those desiring true romantic love.

This response, in effect, reserves romantic love for monogamists exclusively. Those unwilling to observe conventional norms are disqualified from participation in its promises, i.e., romantic love. The hegemonic power monogamy has in mononormative societies extends oppressive forces to those who do not subscribe to its norms by declaring them ineligible or defective. It is relevant that both, the norms upholding monogamy and the ones upholding high tea society in our example leave many people dissatisfied. Doubling down on conventional monogamous norms is harmful in that it deliberately prohibits some people from goods important to their self-conceptions of flourishing.

Another form that practicality defenses take involves appealing to emotions. The thought is that additional relationships tend to be emotionally burdensome. Romantic relationships are "an emotionally demanding task that justifies expecting our partner to concentrate on one partner at a time."[51] Yet, the suppressed assumption here, again, is one that essentializes the emotional demand that romantic relationships must have. This requirement is not immediately clear. Some partners and romantic relationships do not require much emotional demand at all. The recording artists Erykah Badu and Andrè 3000's 2015 song "Hello" captures the sentiment quite perfectly with its lyrics "It's important to me to know that you are free." The artists present the idea that robust autonomous freedom rather than emotional burdening might be an appropriate cornerstone of romantic love. This autonomous freedom is a hallmark of singledom and thus challenges mononormative and amatonormative assumptions in the most fundamental way possible. In addition, some scholars have pointed out that not all non-monogamous relationships involve openness to multiple emotionally intimate relationships at a time.[52]

Aside from treating burdensome emotional intimacy as essential for romantic love, this line of thinking also assumes and thereby imposes a linear trajectory of emotional intimacy. It does not take into account the possibility of fostering emotional intimacy by upholding one's romantic partner's robust autonomous freedom. Instead, the freedom to exist within multiple romantic relationships is treated as something that detracts from, rather than enhances, emotional intimacy in romantic relationships. But for some non-monogamists, such as polyamorists, this is not true.[53] Ultimately, there are a plurality of actions and activities that promote intimacy. For some lovers, playing a hand of cards or sharing music playlists with one another are deeply intimate acts. Expanding our scope to appreciate a fuller range of intimacy-promoting actions or events creates space for much needed conceptual separability such as separating sex from emotional intimacy.[54] For example, some see sex as "conceptually inseparable from the particular kind of emotional intimacy that is associated with erotic love."[55] One reason this association occurs is that sex is thought to be naturally intimate as it is said to "lay one bare psychologically as well as physically."[56] One thing to be said here is that this is a conceptual problem about how someone *conceptualizes* love, intimacy, and sex, not a practical one. This consideration is why Alan Goldman writes "an internal tension is bound to result from an identification of sex…with long-term, deep emotional relationship between two individuals."[57]

In some relationships like friends-with-benefits relationships or even in swinging relationships, the focus can be on sex instead of emotional closeness.[58] In this context, "we can reasonably be confident that the potential for a close emotional bond with another is low, and that the connection is purely or primarily sexual."[59]

Still, one might think that these relationships have a tendency to evolve into deeper, more meaningful relationships. So, while friends-with-benefit relationships and the like, "can't be restricted on practical grounds, couples could have practical reasons to restrict romantically intimate relationships and in turn reasons to restrict sex to romantically intimate relationships."[60] Even if these relationships can and do evolve into more serious relationships where their connection grows to hold an enlarged emotional significance, it is difficult to see how this would hardly justify restricting one's romantic relationship to monogamy. After all, even our emotionally charged non-sexual friendships can be emotionally taxing (and sometimes more so than our romantic relationships) especially when the friendship is a long-standing one. Yet, we do not think of this as a reason to restrict partners from having additional friendships.

There is at least one more version of the TEA defense that focuses on the effects of the constant TEA that one actually *gives* out, instead of emphasizing the limited amount of TEA one *has to give*. This version of the TEA defense—which we might call *an appeal to exhaustion*—focuses on the effects of extending our TEA in multiple relationships. Monogamy thus becomes a mechanism for preserving one's TEA. Some may think that generally love should hardly be as taxing. It is far from clear that monogamy preserves one's TEA. For example, it might well be the case that monogamous relationships are themselves taxing when one or both relata are particularly needy. It's also noteworthy that non-monogamous relationships needn't be thought of as intrinsically *more* laborious than monogamous relationships simply because of their quantitative multiplicity. Recall that the TEA objection emphasizes the fact that we have limited TEA to distribute. Assume with me for the sake of this example that our TEA resources can be quantified; each person has 18 ounces of TEA to pour into any particular relationship they have. It is at least fathomable from this framework that one might align themselves with a relata who takes 18 ounces of TEA; two relata who take 9 ounces of TEA each; or three relata who take 6 ounces of TEA each. In each of these scenarios, the lover would undoubtedly be at capacity. Yet, the multiplicity itself does not immediately show up as cumbersome. In real life, what happens more often than not is that partners do not require us to always function at maximum capacity. Additionally, as I noted earlier, some of the TEA that we have will be distributed toward non-romantic ends. Whether we relate monogamously or non-monogamously, people should instead be encouraged to take an intentional stock of how much TEA they might have to offer any particular relationship. This highlights the fact that instead of relational structure determining how much work a relationship takes, more falls on relata to identify and articulate their relational needs and desires; it's not the relationship, but the people that constitute them. It may be that taking inventory of the relational resources that one has at their disposal does not meet our starry-eyed expectations for what romantic love is or how it looks. But this might suggest that something about our expectations, not the proposed practice has gone awry.

Consent and Non-Monogamy

Patricia Marino has considered strong reasons for challenging the permissibility of consensual non-monogamies, like polyamory.[61] Rightfully so, after all, polyamory is a kind of consensual non-monogamy that places consent at the center of its ethical practice. She alludes to Elizabeth Emens' crucial point that consent is both a practice *and* a value among consensual non-monogamies. Marino appreciates the complexities of "consent" and "non-consent" in practice and wonders whether individual acts of non-monogamies are complicated by these concerns. What happens if one of the relata in a romantic relationship consents for their partner to have sex with someone else, and between the time of consenting and the occurrence of the sex act, changes their mind, she probes. What if the first person consents to some range of agreed-upon activities for their polyamorous relationship, but they engage in different activities instead? Is group consent the same thing as individual consent and how is it determined?

Many of the challenges that consent generates for polyamorous relationships resemble the challenges it generates for sex. To be sure, not all polyamorous relationships are sexual and so thinking about consent does present some unique challenges for polyamory in different varieties. While many polyamory scholars regularly appeal to consent being one of the primary pillars of polyamorous relating, no authors have quite problematized this notion to arrive at an understanding of how this value functions in polyamorous relationships. It may be that polyamorists take consent to perform some kind of "moral magic." But we should not move so quickly to the belief that consent is magical in polyamorous relationships. For example, some psychologists who work with polyamorous partners make the familiar feminist distinction between "true consent" and "coerced consent". How should we understand "true consent" and "coerced consent" in polyamory? Can consent truly neutralize problematic power relationships between relata that may render consent otherwise spurious?

Marino catalogues the historical origins of consent in rape law. This history involves multiple and sometimes competing notions of consent including "no means no"; affirmative consent; and verbal/non-verbal consent. While these various understandings of consent are applied to questions around the legality and moral permissibility of sex, they can be adapted to polyamorous relationships to create peculiar challenges for polyamorists that must be addressed in showing polyamory to be ethically permissible.

Marino notes that common understandings of consent can be sufficiently summed up in a few basic principles—namely, "just do the things that everyone wants, and don't do other things; don't force others to do the things you want; listen to one another, and don't assume your partner shares your own desires."[62] Emens gets a bit more specific and says that the ideal of consent in polyamorous relationships is:

> PC: The partners in a relationship or sexual encounter make an informed decision to participate in the relationship or the encounter including knowing its polyamorous context.[63]

We should notice that Emens' characterization gets a lot right about what consent is for polyamorists. Focusing on her definition of polyamorous consent (PC) will be useful in articulating the challenges consent creates in polyamorous relationships. It can sometimes be a very complicated matter to enact our values in practice. After all, what does it mean to make an "informed decision" in this context? How much information is required to meet this threshold? How should we distinguish true consent from coerced and therefore spurious consent? Marino crafts more specific questions when she explores a series of consent questions (CQs):

CQ1: "What if one person in a committed couple decides that nonmonogamy is something they need to be happy, but the other person wants to be monogamous? No matter what decision they come to, it may be that mutual satisfaction is impossible and that one person feels pressured."[64]

CQ2: "What if one person is married to another non-exclusively, and consents for that person to have sex with a third on some occasion, and then between the time of consenting and the time of sex happening, changes their mind?"[65]

CQ3: "What if the first person consents to some range of activities for their nonexclusive spouse to engage in, but they engage in a different set of activities?"[66]

CQ4: "What if a person consents for their spouse to have sex with others but only if pregnancy is impossible or they use contraception? Contraception can fail. Would the first person be required to help raise the resulting child?"[67]

These questions are pressing enough. Yet reflection on Marino's insights around honesty and communication generates further questions not only about consent but also about privacy. For example, as she rightly notes, some people can be made to feel uncomfortable if their partner shares too much information as the colloquial term "oversharing" denotes:

> CQ5: If there are boundaries around information sharing or disclosure in the relationship, is it plausible that consent can still be garnered? What if one relata desires for there to be a larger degree of information sharing than the other relata is comfortable with?

> CQ6: If a person consents to be in a relationship with another person who is already partnered with someone(s) with robust information sharing policies, in consenting to the relationship is the person consenting to have their information shared with their metamour(s)? What exactly is being consented to when one is consenting to a polyamorous relationship?

> CQ7: Is it enough that consent is given one time? Or must it be continuously given on an ongoing basis?

These questions go beyond an impractical set of "what if's" to arrive at a set of hypotheticals that sometimes actually emerge for polyamorists as Joy Davidson's work suggests.[68] These questions can be separated into four groups by focusing on the worries that appear to motivate them. CQ1 is motivated by concerns of coercion and power; CQs 2 & 7 are underscored by concerns about "contract models of consent"; CQ5 is motivated by concerns about autonomy and the nature of consent; CQs 3, 4, & 6 are motivated by concerns about what is being consented to. Each of these categories (i.e., power & coercion, contract models of consent, autonomy & the nature of consent in polyamory, and informed decision-making) bears on the question of what it means to make an informed decision to participate in a polyamorous relationship.

These concerns do not straightforwardly point to the impermissibility of polyamory. Instead, they critically point to the fact that polyamorous people have duties to themselves (specifically, the duty to know themselves—i.e., their relational needs and desires) and to others (i.e., the duty to specify not only that consent matters but also how it is expected to be communicated). For polyamorists, it is imperative that the duties one has to oneself supervene on the duties that they have to their relata. One way of understanding this comes from Kant's notion of perfect and imperfect duties appearing in The Groundwork.

According to Kant, duties can be separated into at least two kinds: perfect and imperfect duties. Perfect duties, for Kant, highlight the kinds of duties we must always (or never) do (e.g., we must never lie). Imperfect duties, on the other hand, determine our ends or goals (e.g., one must adopt the end of beneficence, or self-perfection, and act accordingly using one's discretion). Further, we have both perfect and imperfect duties to ourselves and others. Deborah Anapol, who is regarded by some as a foundational author on polyamorous literature, discusses the importance of self-knowledge in polyamorous relationships.[69] It is not enough to merely know one's sexual orientation to monogamy as Anapol urges, but also to know one's orientation toward monogamy as well. Polyamorists have a responsibility (i.e., an imperfect duty to themselves) to come to their relationships knowing what they need and desire from their relationship(s) and their partner(s)—practically (i.e., time and attention desired/needed), emotionally, sexually, materially (i.e. financially), and so on. The duty is imperfect because it arises from the hypothetical condition that one desires to participate in a polyamorous relationship. This is what I take Emens to mean when she talks about self-knowledge being a core structural component and the daily substrate of healthy polyamorous relating.[70] What we've been calling the imperfect duty of self-knowledge, illuminates the strong need for constant access to one's own needs, emotions, and desires.

We can also conceive of polyamorists having the imperfect duty to others to specify not only that consent matters but also how it is expected to be communicated. Robin Bauer[71] and Ariane Cruz[72] discuss what some take to be faux pas sexual practices of BDSM. Bauer sees similarities between how people involved with "alternative sex culture" and non-monogamists can create and develop subcultural skills that may function as a guideline for the practice, thereby creating a new morale of negotiation or consensus. Consequentially, this provides the substance for subcultural ethics and the skills required to meet its ethical dictates.

CQs 2, 3, 4, and 6 point to the reality that to establish consent in polyamory, communication and negotiation skills are crucial. To ensure successful negotiation, self-awareness, knowing one's boundaries as well as knowing how to communicate one's desires and limits honestly, are indispensable. The onus is on the relata to negotiate the terms of consent for that relationship. In CQ2, this means relata must know themselves as having a wishy-washy comfortability around their non-exclusive partner's other sexual relationships. Knowing one's self to be this way may reveal the need to accommodate this characteristic about themselves in negotiating what consent will need to look like and what the standards of charitability will be around revoking and withdrawing consent. They may say, "While I am consenting to sex with others being okay, I might change my mind about this at some point and hope there would be space for grace as I struggle with things like this."

Similarly, regarding CQs 3, 4, and 6, the onus is on polyamorists to take stock of as many of the possibilities for their relationship as they can when they are negotiating the parameters of consent for said relationship. This is perhaps the best practice for polyamorists who desire to limit ambiguity around key relational values and responsibilities.

It may be as Bauer warns, that the onus placed on polyamorists to negotiate what consent will look like in the context of their relationships eliminates much of the spontaneity (read as "fun"), passion, or eroticism that lie within the transgression of the limits of reason. These elements are sometimes thought to be crucial to romantic relationships. However, Niko Kolodny[73] and Gabriele Taylor[74] depict love's responsiveness to reason and cast doubt on the centrality and cruciality of these elements for romantic love.

There are two related concerns. On one hand, one might wonder whether this negotiation model of consent sets an unreasonably high bar or is too rigid for practitioners of polyamory. On the other hand, one might wonder with Lois Pineau whether this negotiation model treats our romantic relationships (and their associated responsibilities) too much like a contract in which garnering consent is a one-time act.[75]

Regarding the thought that the negotiation model sets a high bar for polyamorists, perhaps it does. Aristotle's insights around excellence come to mind and they are relevant here. For Aristotle, excellence requires a kind of precision. As a result, "there are many ways of going astray (for the bad belongs to what is unlimited…the good to what is limited), whereas there is only one way of getting it right (which is exactly why the one is easy and the other difficult); … for single and straight is the road of the good; the bad go bad every which way."[76] Polyamory is kind of like this. Polyamory and being polyamorous can be an extremely challenging undertaking precisely because there are so many ways of getting it wrong. This is reflected in the infinite enumerability of possibilities that polyamorists attribute to polyamory. If the standards of polyamorous practice are seemingly high to meet, it is because they are. Love and loving relationships are serious matters. Although she is most likely speaking about monogamous relationships, Diane Enns' account of love describes the risks inherently intertwined with romantic love.[77] There is often a lot at stake, including one's own physical, emotional/mental, and moral well-being. These risks (and the possibilities for harm) become exacerbated when more relata are added to the equation. Different people will interpret harms and pleasures differently. No matter how difficult or challenging the responsibility one has for self-knowledge, for polyamorists it is a necessary pre-condition for negotiation. The bar is high and polyamorists must do their best to meet it.

The concern over rigidity has semblances with the concern that wonders whether the negotiation model treats romantic relationships too much like contracts. Signing contracts typically binds us to the terms of the agreement at the outset. That is, there usually is no space to renegotiate the terms of a contract once it is signed. Contracts, it is thought, are therefore incompatible with love relationships because relationships are fluid and they ebb and flow. Relationships and relata are dynamic. What if a person's emotions, needs, or desires change throughout the relationship? What if what was once necessary for the well-being of the relationship (e.g., certain kinds of disclosures), is no longer necessary? Importantly,

Marino notes that sometimes contracts are nullified if they are found to have been made under coercion, pressure, or duress for example.

We should think of consent in polyamory as a kind of mutual and ongoing process of negotiation (arriving at mutually accepted terms from time to time). This conception is flexible enough to accommodate changes in relata and relationship dynamics. Michelle Anderson's negotiation model based on verbal consent is useful here.[78] She describes the negotiation process as requiring "consultation, reciprocal communication, and the exchange of views... communication that is verbal unless partners have established a context between them in which they may accurately assess one another's non-verbal behavior... [and] [t]he verbal communication must be such as would indicate to a reasonable person" prior to engaging in the penetrative sex act in question.[79] I believe that Anderson's account can be extended beyond penetrative sex acts to romantic acts more broadly. That is, the negotiation process for participating in polyamorous relationships reflects the negotiation process outlined by Anderson where the activity in question is (ongoing) participation in the polyamorous relationship and its polyamorous contexts. The negotiation model speaks directly to CQ7—consent is continuously given on an ongoing basis unless otherwise established by the relata in that relationship.

The negotiation model also speaks to CQ5 directly. Consent can still plausibly be garnered in relationships even if there are boundaries around information sharing. In a negotiation, relata can express their discomforts around certain kinds of disclosures or information sharing to establish what consent will look like in the context of that relationship and what is needed for the relata to be comfortable. For example, suppose that while A consents to B engaging in extradyadic sexual relationships (suppose further that A consents to the widest range of sex acts possible), A is uncomfortable with hearing about B's sexcapades. A and B might consent to a "don't ask don't tell" policy around which this information will be disclosed to A only in the case that A asks. As Ritchie and Barker remind us, polyamorists are regularly engaged in constructing unique language for themselves in a culture of compulsory monogamy. Alternatively, A and B can create language around these kinds of disclosures that do not activate A's discomfort; for example, instead of saying "Hey A, I am going to have/just had sex with C", B can say, "Hey A, I am "going to the bakery" this weekend" where "going to the bakery" communicates what it needs to communicate about B's other relationships, potentially without upsetting A or making them uncomfortable.

This is not foolproof. A's discomfort might just as easily be activated. Or B might have a stronger desire to share with A about their relationship with C, for the sake of fostering a more robust intimacy with A. I must emphasize here that the purpose of negotiation is not to eradicate risks from romantic relationships. I am skeptical that any device we use to understand the ethicality of romantic relationships can do this. But perhaps it is most useful to simply note that romantic relationships, whether between two relata or more, require cooperation and sometimes compromise. We seldom are able to get everything that we desire from our romantic relationships (thank goodness for our friends!). The expectation that we should is less reasonable than expecting relata to know themselves as a pre-condition for romantic relating. The impact of these compromises tells a story about the cost of cooperation in our relationships, but this is no reason to fret. Finally, I seriously question whether the burden on polyamorists to present a foolproof plan for eradicating risk in romantic relationships is unreasonably lofty; especially as it is far from clear that any device (monogamous or otherwise) can achieve this.

As this section shows, while polyamorous relationships centralize consent, there are some challenges regarding it. I endeavored to show that the negotiation model can meet most of these challenges—namely CQs 2–7. In the next section, I show how the negotiation model meets the issue that I take to be at the heart of CQ1 and related concerns.

Spurious Consent

CQ1 asks: What if one person in a committed couple decides that nonmonogamy is something they need to be happy, but the other person wants to be monogamous? No matter what decision they come to, it may be that mutual satisfaction is impossible and that one person feels pressured.

The emphasis here reveals the heart of the concern: oppression, coercion, and duress. One might caution that we should be wary of spurious consent. Choices that are made under oppressive conditions consequently perpetuate unequal power relations. As such, in asymmetrical power relationships, consent for the party with less power may be constrained and therefore not genuine (especially in the absence of other viable options). Gregg Strauss has openly questioned whether plural relationships are inherently unequal.[80] As Emens notes, however, challenges dealing with problematic asymmetric power relationships are usually about polygamy and not polyamory.

Strauss is occupied with the question of whether there can be a morally acceptable ideal of polygamous marriage. On his view, polygamy is morally objectionable because it precludes genuine equality between spouses. Further, he thinks that these inequalities are structurally built into polygamy. Strauss does not conflate polygamy with polygyny but says that "most polygamist communities discriminate based on gender and sexuality by permitting only polygyny. Men may marry multiple women, but women may not marry multiple men, and no one may marry someone of the same sex."[81] The gender dynamics are relevant because current plural relationships are accompanied by a sexist culture and gender hierarchical power relationships.

We should note with Emens, that in comparison to polygamy, polyamory at least in principle eschews gendered hierarchies and encompasses a wider range of intimate relationships between more than two people. These relationships include gay and lesbian relationships where, though power may still be asymmetrically distributed along the lines of class or race, for example, it may be neutral along gendered lines. Still, differential power dynamics between men and women, especially in cultures where heterosexuality is compulsory, might create problems for women and polyamorous relationships.

If, generally speaking, women lack the requisite power for consent because of how they are positioned socially and politically then Strauss is right to question whether women voluntarily choose these relationships. We should point out, however, that it is unclear how monogamy would rectify these dynamics. More than a question about the permissibility of polyamory, this would generate more pressing questions about the permissibility of heterosexual relationships with any number of partners. It is perhaps more useful to point out that Andrew Samuels has discussed how the practice of "switching" in consensual D/S[82] sexual dynamics reveal a capacity for an individual to be powerful in one sphere of life and less powerful in another.[83] "Switches" are people who sometimes prefer to occupy dominant positions and other times prefer to occupy submissive positions of power in erotic space. Through negotiation, switches can negotiate which of these positions of power they will occupy in erotic space (often called "scenes" by BDSM/kink practitioners). Ariane Cruz discusses how these kinds of negotiations contain possibilities for liberation and empowerment for Black women BDSMers and kinksters who engage in "race play".[84]

Similarly, the negotiation process contains the potential to neutralize asymmetrical power dynamics in establishing polyamorous relationships as well, such that someone less powerful in one sphere of life can be made more powerful in another—namely, the polyamorous relationship(s). Even more, we might share Den Otter's skepticism questioning symmetrical power relations as a requisite for the legitimation of consent. This may set the bar too high. It is more reasonable for members of a diverse and free society to accept "that many people will make less than full autonomous choices because of the beliefs they have acquired—notwithstanding their rationality"[85] and this may just be good enough or as good as subjects in ideologically compromised liberal societies (e.g., racist, sexist, homophobic, transphobic, misogynist, misandrist, classist, etc.) can do.

There is a different, but related problem for polyamorous relationships. Much of what has been said so far has considered polyamorous relationships through the lens of individuals negotiating with other individuals dyadically (i.e., a 1:1 ratio). But sometimes polyamorous relationships include an individual negotiating with groups—such as a "unicorn" or someone who desires to engage with a couple sexually or romantically. This consideration prompts another question:

> CQ8: Is group consent the same as individual consent? What if one member of a polycule is outnumbered on some practical, political, or ideological decision needing to be made involving their group relationship?

Undoubtedly, this is a distinct problem from the problem of gendered hierarchies. It instead asks about the navigation of intimate relationships when the dominant possession of power over the relationship(s) resides in a smaller subgroup contained within the larger relationship(s). How are these decisions to be made? Can fairness be achieved for everyone involved? Surely, the threat of coercion or duress is intensified where these kinds of dynamics are present.

The negotiation process does not wither here. Instead, it takes stock of this possibility as one needed to be accounted for in establishing what the terms or boundaries of one's relationship will be. Questions of shared governance have been discussed at length to no consensus. Questions about shared governance are at the heart of Plato's *Republic*, Aristotle's *Politics*, and John Rawls' *Theory of Justice*, for example. Thoroughgoing explorations of democracy, oligarchy, tyranny, etc. as polyamorous politics may be useful in future research. However, to think through fair distributive principles or address whether any of these forms of governance emerge as universally preferable for polyamories takes us beyond the scope of this project. I am a pluralist about value when it comes to governing practices of polyamories. Different things are required for different polycules—what traumas are the particular relata bringing to the relationship? What things are being desired and requested? It may be that some polyamorous people elect for more equitable democratic processes, while others opt for more hierarchical models of power distribution. Some relata may prefer to govern by majority rules and others by unanimity. Proverbially, "different strokes work for different folks."

It is best to reemphasize the importance of the knowledge of one's own needs and desires when negotiating the terms of their relationship involvement. By way of best practices, perhaps it is ideal to discuss how the relata will navigate conflicts as they are designing their relationships. To require this, however, is unreasonable insofar as people generally do not know what they do not know. Notwithstanding the inability to anticipate the unknown, relata should at the very least do the best they can to extend grace to one another and revisit their negotiation process as these instances emerge on a case-by-case basis.

Eve Rickert, the co-author of *More than Two* and co-founder of Thorntree Press (perhaps the most prominent press on polyamorous works) questions the ethicality of polyamorous hierarchies in a 2016 blog post.[86] Rickert asks whether a polyamorous hierarchy—defined as at least one relata holding more power over another relata's other relationships than is held by the people within those relationships—can be ethical. She writes "In poly relationships, control can also manifest through hierarchical agreements where partners give each other the power to make unilateral decisions over other relationships...Usually, in hierarchical agreements, the rules are presented to secondary partners as a take-it-or-leave-it proposition, without an opportunity to shape their creation—either in the beginning, or in the future."[87] Among some polyamorous subcultures, there is an expressed distaste for dating "spouses" or dating couples more broadly. Rickert cautions that the consequences of relationship hierarchies might result in not dating someone you may want to date, putting the brakes on a relationship that's growing too fast, or it may "affect your decision whether to be poly at all" in less extreme cases and in more extreme cases, may result in physical or emotional abuse. The threat of abuse in polyamorous relationships is underscored by social workers and trauma-informed polyamorist advocates such as Alicia Bunyan-Sampson (also known as "@PolyamorousBlackGirl").

As we have already seen, sometimes individuals can consent to reduce their power in relationships.[88] Agreeing to participate in hierarchical polyamorous relationships needn't be problematic. Sometimes people prefer for their partners to make decisions about the relationship(s) (e.g., where and when they might go on dates, what they will eat for dinner, what cities they will live in, etc.). It makes sense that sometimes people forfeit their right to make certain relational decisions. In these cases, whether they are forfeiting this right to individual relata or forfeiting it to a partner's relationship with another partner, it should be discussed as a part of their negotiation process.

There is a worry about whether these kinds of relationship dynamics are themselves compulsory. Non-monogamist writers often discuss "couples' privilege" where the large and asymmetrically distributed power is reserved for the socially sanctioned "couple". If couples are, by default, more powerful than the individual, then we run into the same kinds of consent problems as we did around gender difference earlier. Namely, it would be questionable whether or not an individual could ever give consent from such unequal negotiating positions—an individual's agency would always be eclipsed by the powers vested in the couple. Even if one knows themselves and is aware of themselves as agents, they may still be prone to participating in polyamorous relationships with unfair or abusive dynamics.

Sociologist Elizabeth Sheff's work points out that polyamorous units can sometimes have the opposite effects on polyamorists:

> While [intimate partner violence] is obviously a problem in some poly relationships, polys can use their contacts with multiple partners and social networks to ameliorate some of its impacts when it does happen…people in poly relationships might be less likely to experience [intimate partner violence] because they are more connected to more people and thus potentially much harder to isolate. Multiple partners provide additional social resources that can help polys leave abusive relationships…It makes sense that people might hesitate to abuse their partners… in front of other people simply for the well-deserved shame of it. The presence of another person may not only embarrass the potential abuser but it may also shift the balance of power and that person might be able to physically intervene on behalf of the partner who is being attacked.[89]

Through Sheff's lens, there will be some polyamorous relationship dynamics where intimate partner violence and abuse is less likely. It also shows how balances of power can shift when the least powerful party can appeal to other relata in the relationship. Having relational power concentrated in a subrelational majority is therefore Janus-faced—there are some cases where it may go poorly and other cases where it may go well.

Given that polyamory allows for a potentially infinite number of relational dynamics, it is grossly impractical to try to evaluate each possible dynamic. What the concerns about being outnumbered in a relationship in ways that constrain one's agency show are that perhaps some polyamorous dynamics should be avoided and not that polyamory should be avoided altogether. To avoid concerns about coercion and spurious consent, polyamorists have a responsibility to be as clear as they can in articulating what the relational boundaries will be and what those boundaries imply. This responsibility is borne out of the fact that in amatonormative and mononormative societies where monogamy is the default way of understanding relationships, polyamorists must develop new morals as guidelines for their personal practice and its ethical dictates. To be sure, this responsibility for polyamorists emerges from amatonormativity and mononormativity in ways that it does not for their monogamous counterparts. It is worth questioning whether the state has responsibilities (i.e., equal treatment) to polyamorous persons to undo the culture of compulsory monogamy so that undue burdens on polyamorists are lifted. I think that it does, but we will discuss that in more detail in Chapter 4.

Polyamory is Harmful to the Society

To this point, we have largely considered harms at the level of the individual such as coercion and abuse. Some opponents of polyamory opt for a slightly different strategy. Because some people associate polyamory with divorce and with the breakdown of families, there exists the thought that polyamory is harmful to the very fabric of society.[90]

Sheff's work extends beyond considering the impacts on the adult members of polyamorous relationships and their relationship dynamics to focus on understanding polyamorous families. What proponents of this argument have in mind when making this objection to polyamory is the idea of the nuclear family—one rooted in heterosexuality, mononormativity, and amatonormativity. In Sheff's view, some Western cultures suffer from this fascination with the idyllic vision of marriage and romantic love. For her, this fascination gives rise to epistemic fabrications that "families used to be static institutions that never evolved and only began to change with the sexual revolution of the 1960s" resulting in "the false impression that families today are caught in an unprecedented state of chaos."[91] Changes in labor markets and other social institutions have shown families to be a shifting institution. For example, some sociologists highlight the fact that in the U.S., shifts in gender norms, marital relationships, and the family occurred as women's participation in the labor force grew.[92] The thought here is that as women became more able to make a living for themselves outside of the role of the "housewife", they were afforded more possibilities of being and becoming that did not include conceiving of themselves as mere wives and mothers. Sheff ties women's proliferation in the labor force to an increase in divorce and the subsequent creation of "blended families and serial monogamy, and the increase in single parenthood through divorce and non-marital childbirth."[93]

The argument that polyamorous relationships break families down and are therefore harmful to the very fabric of society contains central assumptions that might be questioned. First, it unjustifiably assumes the nuclear family as its paradigm.

This assumption fails to take stock of not only the blended families resulting from serial monogamy that Sheff mentions, but also the social reality of chosen families and kinships—it assumes that they do not nor cannot exist. Families established by fostering, adoption, careful kinship selectivity, or different or same-sex relationships where children are not desired are reduced to second class. Further, according to Eleanor Wilkinson, more people are participating in alternative family structures and communal living at our present moment than ever before.[94] Instead of asking whether polyamorous families might exist and how, by default, the assumption leaves no room for this possibility. As the interviews contained in Sheff's work demonstrate, however, these families do exist. Yet the assumption prevents us from asking the question of how polyamorous families might aid or viably contribute to enhancing our social fabric.

An opponent may think that this is not the fairest way to respond to this objection. They might say that the point is not that polyamorous families *do* exist, but whether they *should*. How we go about answering these questions should take stock not only of the challenges that polyamorous families uniquely present, but also of the potential benefits that these families might contribute to our social fabric in ways that are not detrimental to it. If, as it turns out that the challenges can be met, we would have even more reason for thinking that non-monogamies like polyamory are ethically permissible.

Generally speaking, we might think of families as involving complex dynamics between and among their members. Adding more people and relational dynamics only serves to complicate these relationships further. After all, polyamorous relationships may not last permanently in their original form. For example, we might think that "In monogamous relationships that end, people usually do not have to deal with someone close to them continuing to date someone with whom they have just ended a relationship."[95] "And what about the children?!," we might say, routine family challenges like jealousy among siblings can be exacerbated when intensified by polyamorous dynamics. Furthermore, is it reasonable for us to expect children to be able to adapt to so many different parenting styles? Doesn't polyamory set the stage for children to become attached to "parents" who are related by the unstable bonds of polyamorous relationships?

It is worth pointing out that polyamorous families do not merely exist, some of them thrive. While opponents point out that polyamorous relationships may not be stable in the permanent sense, Sheff's work on polyamorous families challenges permanence as a monolithic relational value. She's found that "some poly relationships appear more durable than monogamous relationships because their flexibility allows them to meet shifting needs over time in a way that monogamous relationships—with their abundant norms and requirements of sexual fidelity—find more challenging."[96]

Whether the alleged instability of polyamorous families is *necessarily* detrimental is far from a settled question. Den Otter urges that the arguments against multi-party relationships on the grounds of whether these dynamics are detrimental to child welfare need considerably more evidence. He writes "It may not take an entire village to raise a child, but it stands to reason that all things being equal, parental multiplicity may be even more conducive to meeting children's needs. Indeed, it may turn out that on average, the existence of more than two caregivers is the superior parenting arrangement."[97] Instead, the fluidity of multi-party parenting styles presents new possibilities for children for instance, "…having more

than one "father" or "mother" as caregivers would not necessarily undermine the welfare of children. Children may be
loved and nurtured in unconventional families, provided that
their caregivers have the necessary skills and the motivation to
use them. They may benefit from having more than two adults
to talk to about their lives and receive advice."[98] Generally,
Den Otter thinks the usual arguments leveraged against multi-
party parenting dynamics do not consider the possibilities
that multi-parent arrangements could be a superior parenting
framework compared to the two-parent model or that even if
all things are not equal, in the real world, the alternatives may
be worse.[99] There is also the possibility that children can be
protected directly from harm in ways that do not centralize
the nuclear family—i.e., through public policy.

Some of the challenges that aim at polyamorous families
implicitly assume that polyamorists are attempting to impose
a universal standard of parenting and families. Rambukkana
mentions how polyamorous organizations are sometimes
interpreted as recruitment machines that suck people in
with the promises of sex and more sex due to their having
unbalanced views of sex and relationships. We should be
mindful of the fact that the advocation for polyamorous families is not the same thing as arguing for the universalization
of polyamorous families. I should also point out with Den
Otter and others, that the universalizability of monogamous
families is itself unclear. Highlighting some of the virtues of
multi-party families does little to undermine the social and
political co-existence of the nuclear family.

While the universalizability argument is one that lay outside of the scope of our current inquiry, some preliminary
remarks can be delightfully insightful here. The challenge or
threat that polyamory poses of deteriorating the social fabric

might be leveraged differently. It could be that the harm done to society by polyamory is found in the consideration that it does not pass the 'universalizability' test. Kant talks very conservatively about sex and relationships, albeit not in the language of the universal law. For Kant, marriage was a way of satisfying a moral condition for permissible sex between persons.[100] Seemingly preoccupied with thinking about how we might ethically satisfy our sexual impulses, in some places such as his *Metaphysics of Morals*, Kant can be found saying a variety of objectionable things pertaining to sexuality and sexual relationships (i.e., on matters involving masturbation, homosexuality, and sexual reproduction). But what about the universalizability test?[101]

Perhaps we could stipulate a kind of procedure where we ask if the maxim is that I will have more than one partner when I feel that it meets my needs. Suppose further we ask whether we could imagine that everyone act on this reason all the time. Can we will this maxim? There does not seem to be a contradiction here so long as the partner you are pursuing also reserves the space for pursuing other partners of their own. The next step for us would be to ask ourselves whether we would want to live in this kind of world. Even though there is no contradiction here, we may not want to live in a world like that. We might instead think, however, that the universalizability test with non-monogamy gets us closer to the kingdom of ends. As we work our way through this decision procedure, conceiving of a society where everyone is open to polyamory is advantageous for monogamies and non-monogamies alike. For example, in that world perhaps the pernicious nature of stigma and resistance to polyamory would be reduced and thereby create more room for tolerance and understanding of difference.

SUMMARY

When we began this chapter, we aimed at the question of whether it was okay to be non-monogamous. We surveyed common arguments rejecting polyamory. These included monogamous naturalism, divine ordination, the defense from specialness, the jealousy defense, the defense from sexual health, and the TEA objection. Each of these defenses come up short of fully justifying monogamy. Far from showing that the only morally permissible romantic love relationships are monogamous ones, many of the defenses on offer can be extended to non-monogamies.

The chapter also argued that consent generates challenges that span issues of power, privilege, and positionality. I explored what consent can mean for polyamorists and how it might be understood in polyamorous relationships. While polyamory does not definitively resolve consent questions, insights from subaltern sexual practices reveal useful models for how consent might be negotiated across asymmetrical positions of power.

Requiring definitive conclusions from polyamorists presents a high bar for them to meet and one that is not straightforwardly shared by their monogamous counterparts. Finally, I explored arguments that polyamory is detrimental to the social fabric. There is some evidence available on polyamories that suggest that instead of polyamory being detrimental to the social fabric, polyamorous families create new possibilities for rethinking what families are and how we should think about them.

REFERENCES

Anapol, Deborah M. *Polyamory the New Love Without Limits: Secrets of sustainable intimate relationships*. IntiNet Resource Center, 1997.

Anderson, Michelle J. "Negotiating Sex." *Southern California Law Review* 78 (2005): 101.

Bauer, Robin. "Non-Monogamy in Queer BDSM communities: Putting the sex back into alternative relationship practices and discourse." in *Understanding Non-monogamies*, ed. Meg Barker and Darren Langdridge, 154–165. Routledge, 2010.

Broadie, Sarah, and Christopher Rowe. Eds. *Nicomachean Ethics*. Oxford University Press, 2002.

Brunning, Luke. "Compersion: An Alternative to Jealousy?," *Journal of the American Philosophical Association* 6, no. 2 (2020): 225–245.

Chalmers, Harry. "Is Monogamy Morally Permissible?." *The Journal of Value Inquiry* 53, no.2 (2019): 225–241.

Cooper, John M., and Douglas S. Hutchinson, eds. *Plato: Complete works*. Hackett Publishing, 1997.

Cruz, Ariane. *The Color of Kink*. NYU Press, 2016.

Davidson, Joy. "Working with polyamorous clients in the clinical setting." *Electronic Journal of Human Sexuality* 5, no. 8 (2002): 465.

Den Otter, Ronald C. *In Defense of Plural Marriage*. Cambridge University Press, 2015.

Emens, Elizabeth F. "Monogamy's Law: Compulsory Monogamy and Polyamorous Existence." *NYU Rev. L. & Soc. Change* 29 (2004): 277.

Fern, Jessica. *Polysecure: Attachment, trauma and consensual nonmonogamy*. Thorntree Press LLC, 2020.

Frankfurt, Harry G. *The Reasons of Love*. Princeton University Press, 2009.

George, Robert, Sherif Girgis and Ryan T. Anderson. "The Argument Against Gay Marriage: And Why It Doesn't Fail." Accessed December 30, 2021. www.thepublicdiscourse.com/2010/12/2217/.

Goldman, Alan H. "Plain Sex," *Philosophy & Public Affairs* (1977): 267–287.

Jenkins, Carrie. *What Love Is: And what it could be*. Basic Books, 2017.

Marino, Patricia. *Philosophy of Sex and Love: An opinionated introduction*. Routledge, 2019.

McMurtry, John. "Monogamy: A critique." *The Monist* (1972): 587–599.

Niko Kolodny. "Love as Valuing a Relationship." *The Philosophical Review* 112, no. 2 (2003): 135–189.

Pineau, Lois. "Date rape: A feminist analysis." *Law and Philosophy* 8, no. 2 (1989): 217–243.

Rickert, Eve. "Can Polyamorous hierarchies be ethical? Part 1: The tower and the village." Accessed December 31, 2021, https://brighterthansunflowers.com/2016/06/10/can-polyamorous-hierarchies-ethical-part-1-tower-village/.

Samuels, Andrew. "Promiscuities: Politics, imagination, spirituality and hypocrisy." in *Understanding Non-monogamies*, ed. Meg Barker and Darren Langdridge, 212–221. Routledge, 2010.

Séguin, Léa J. "The good, the bad, and the ugly: Lay attitudes and perceptions of polyamory." *Sexualities* 22, no. 4 (2019).

Sheff, Elisabeth. *The Polyamorists Nextdoor: Inside multiple-partner relationships and families* Rowman & Littlefield.

Strauss, Gregg. "Is Polygamy Inherently Unequal?." *Ethics* 122, no. 3 (2012).

Taylor, Gabriele. "Love." in *Proceedings of the Aristotelian Society* 76, no. 1 (1976).

Weaver, Bryan R., and Fiona Woollard. "Marriage and the Norm of Monogamy." *The Monist* 9, no. 3–4 (2008): 506–522.

Wlikinson, Eleanor, "What's queer about non-monogamy now," in *Understanding Non-monogamies*, ed. Meg Barker and Darren Langdridge, 243–254. Routledge, 2010.

York, Kyle. "Why monogamy is morally permissible: a defense of some common justifications for monogamy." *The Journal of Value Inquiry* (2019): 1–14.

Three

MONOGAMOUS IDENTITY?

For some people monogamy provides an identity label; they speak of monogamy as something they *are* rather than something that they *believe* or *do*. For example, people comfortably say that they "are monogamous" even in periods where they are single or infideletous. Throughout the literature on sexuality and love, monogamy has sometimes appeared in discussions around sexual and romantic orientation.[1] Ritchie and Barker see the emergence of romantic identities belonging to trends of groups claiming rights and citizenship based on their sexual or relational identities.[2]

There is something to this point. The work of legal historians such as John Witte, Jr. and legal theorists like Ann Tweedy, have shed a strong light on how monogamy and people's standing as "monogamous" mediate rulings in legal proceedings about citizenship and immigration, child custody, religious freedom, and discrimination.[3] In 2020, amidst a global pandemic, Canada's Minister of Immigration, Refugees, and Citizenship announced that romantic partners would be allowed to cross the border to see their loved ones, so long as they were in an "exclusive [read as dyadic] dating relationship".[4] American institutions, especially marriage,

DOI: 10.4324/9781003375036-4

legally prioritize and incentivize monogamous intimate relationships at the expense of other meaningful relationships. Rights and privileges are mediated through how one is positioned concerning monogamous norms. It makes sense that those who are routinely marginalized for deviating from these norms might appeal to a kind of identity politics to protect themselves socially and politically. However, we will set this aside for now and return to it later on.

Given the ways that monogamy dominates our social and political landscape (i.e., mononormativity and amatonormativity), there are several reasons people identify themselves as monogamous. Socially, stigma and shame attach to practices that are non-monogamous and this cannot be understated. Men and women who deviate from monogamous norms are treated as pariahs and publicly shamed by being labeled "players", "sluts", "hoochies", "hoes", "jezebels", "home-wreckers", "sex-craved", etc.[5] Identifying as monogamous (even in the case that one is not presently in a monogamous relationship, e.g., "singles") then, offers a particular kind of protection from social castigation. Further, politically speaking, identifying as monogamous preserves one's claim (read as "entitlement") to the bundle of privileges and rights under marriage at some point in their life (so long as marriage continues to protect the monogamous dyad exclusively).

On my view monogamy is not, strictly speaking, an identity. However, we needn't reject the assumption that such an identity can exist. There is a rationale that helps us make sense of monogamous identity in a conventional sense. For example, Tweedy and Samuel Macrosson have discussed the notion of 'embeddedness' when talking about various identity types. Probing the viability of polyamorous sexual identity, Tweedy follows a theory of embeddedness (that she attributes to Macrosson) where "The more embedded a way of being is the more sense it makes to consider it an identity and specifically a sexual orientation."[6]

On this view, identities exist on a spectrum ranging from most to least embedded. On the most embedded end of the spectrum are "essential identities" (assuming that such identities could exist). Very close to essential identities would be identities that are socio-culturally constructed and are "so constraining and powerful that individuals would live their assignment to one classification rather than another as wholly unchosen and unchangeable."[7] On the other end of the spectrum—the least embedded identities—are those that are "experienced as wholly extraneous to [one's] identit[y]."[8]

I suggest that monogamous identities are socio-culturally constructed through *resonances*, and could fall along various points of this spectrum. Among the most embedded would be individuals for whom *all* conventional monogamy's associated beliefs (i.e., i.-iv. from Chapter 1) *deeply resonate* with in a way they believe to be essential to them; or, at least, resonate with them in a way that they believe to be so constraining and powerful that their assignment to "monogamy" appears unchosen and unchangeable. At other points, we might find individuals for whom only some of monogamy's beliefs resonate with them; or that some beliefs resonate more than or instead of others (e.g., sexual exclusivity instead of emotional exclusivity). Toward the least embedded end of the spectrum, we might find people who do not identify as monogamists, but whose romantic relationships adhere to monogamous tenants. For them, monogamy might be experienced as wholly extraneous as it is likely they would be identified from the outside as "monogamists" (i.e., by their family, friends, and fellow members of society).

Suffice it to say that resonances *track* embeddedness and embeddedness *reflects* resonances. To borrow an example from Tweedy, imagine an individual who takes the bus to work out of necessity and another who does so regularly as an expression of deep-seated environmentalism. In the former case, "the bus-taking would be at the far extreme of casual or superficial identity", while for the latter "the same activity would fall somewhere in the middle between the two poles because being a bus-taker would likely be a designation that the individual associated herself with and was proud of."[9] The thought here would be that the beliefs constituting being a "bus-taker" would more deeply resonate with the second person rather than the first.[10]

The more embedded an identity is, the more likely it would be to manifest as strong and consistent (or rather stable and unchanging); this is true even if the identity turns out to be mutable. The depth of resonance will usually track the degree of embeddedness that one experiences. As beliefs belonging to the monogamous convention wane, so too then will the sense in which one experiences that identity as embedded. Conventional identities, such as monogamy, are mutable insofar as their beliefs may or may not resonate with individuals who belong to the culture the convention is a part of.

One thing that falls out of thinking of monogamous identity in terms of embeddedness, is not only the mutability of monogamy but also of romantic identities more broadly. That is, the same person can identify as monogamous, non-monogamous, or even romantically ambiguous, at different points in their lives. This, of course, hinges on the degree that beliefs belonging to cultural conventions resonate with the individual's identity in question.

It is important to understand that resonances are contained within the scope of an individual's beliefs—and more specifically, what they take themselves to believe.[11] It is not the case, in other words, that resonance will always motivate an individual to act consistently with what they take themselves to believe. Take a serial cheater for example. The serial cheater may identify as a "monogamist" despite behavior reflecting an inability to adhere to the monogamous convention. Some may think that we ought to question whether the conventional beliefs *actually* resonate with this individual, irrespective of their self-reports. However, I presuppose that individuals are discrete and autonomous entities who reserve the power for identifying themselves and believe it is better practice to support them in doing so. This is what is meant by the age-old adage, "When someone tells you who they are, believe them."

Whatever the dissonance (if it may be called that) that a serial cheater experiences would make sense given the ways that monogamous ideologies are imposed and disseminated throughout Western culture. Given the prevalence of amatonormativity and mononormativity, we could reasonably expect them to shape an individual's perceptions "so deeply that the reality is, to the individual" that monogamy is their identity and that it is unchangeable. To understand this is to understand the position of hegemonic dominance that monogamy occupies.

Our discussion of monogamous identity now presents an opportunity to explore amatonormativity and mononormativity in a bit more detail. Both amatonormativity and mononormativity are sustained by mechanisms that are social and political. Politically, the institution of marriage functions to sanction which intimate relationships are valid and worthy of legal protection. Elizabeth Emens writes, "Norms strongly urge people toward monogamy, and law contributes to that pressure in various ways…namely criminal adultery laws, bigamy laws, marriage laws, custody cases, workplace discrimination, and zoning laws."[12] In the United States, there are at least 1,138 statutory provisions that treat marital status as a determining factor in who receives rights, privileges, and other associated benefits.[13] Thus, the institution of marriage is the fulcrum upon which political privilege swings and a site where power is accrued and disseminated. Socially, various contemporary forms of media, especially in print, song, and film, often present dyadic monogamy as the romantic ideal with no alternatives.[14] To say that dyadic monogamy is presented with little to no alternatives is not the strictest way of speaking. Non-monogamies make appearances as the demonized opposite of monogamy. Thus, the dominant representation of dyadic monogamy in media is not normatively neutral; it contains moralistic evaluations of intimate romantic relationships and the people in them. In part, this is why we believe it's okay to be monogamous. As the age-old K-I-S-S-I-N-G rhyme reminds us, first comes (dyadic) love, then comes marriage, and then comes the baby in the baby carriage.[15]

Writers in a number of places have described monogamy as compulsory. Return with me for just a moment to the serial cheater. The power and prevalence of dyadism via amatonormativity and mononormativity, provide some explanation of what might be happening in the case of someone who identifies as monogamous but cheats habitually. Independent of what one's actual desires for intimate romantic relationships are, individuals are culturally conditioned to think about romance and romantic relationships through the lens most readily available to them; in this case, this lens is one of dyadic monogamy. Serial cheaters, in other words, may identify as monogamists (or, with monogamy) not because their own innermost desires correspond to the tenants of monogamy, but because of an oversaturated exposure to dyadic monogamy. This may, in turn, result in a weak residual resonance(s) with its tenants (even if merely through mimicry or wanton repetition). Yet, given the mutability of romantic identity on the embedded-ness account, we could reasonably expect that with more exposure to alternative ways of existing in intimate romantic relationships, a serial cheater may find that the conventional beliefs associated with non-monogamy more deeply resonate with them (as may be the case among former serial cheaters turned ethical non-monogamists).

Non-Monogamous Identity(-ies)

Much like monogamy does for some, "non-monogamy" also provides an identity label for some people. It is not uncommon to come across "Ethical Non-monogamists", "Polyamorists", "Swingers", or "Polygamists" being used as identifying markers—as something people *are* rather than as something they *do*. As such, there is a discourse that mirrors the discourses had around monogamous identities. But insofar as non-monogamy is a social convention that is derived from monogamy, non-monogamy is not, strictly speaking, an identity either. In what follows, I provide a rationale for thinking about how non-monogamous identities function. I maintain, much as I do for monogamous identities, that romantic identities are socially constructed and filter our experience of the world and how we understand our own and others' ways of relating intimately.

We should expect conventional references to non-monogamy as an identity to work in a way where "the more embedded a way of being is, the more sense it makes to consider it an identity."[16] On my view, non-monogamous identities are socially constructed through resonances and fall along various points of the non/monogamy spectrum. In other words, romantic identities track the degree to which socially conventional beliefs resonate with a person. Ritchie and Barker consider the ways that polyamorous people use language to "make sense of identities, relationships, and emotions that fall outside of the dominant cultural constructions of love and relationships."[17] Their work adds texture to how we interact with our socio-linguistic landscape to make sense of ourselves and create organizing principles for communities of people whose lived experiences with intimate relationships and sexuality deviate from well-established social norms. As these communities understand that "claim[ing] community, rights, and recognition"[18] requires a clear social and political legibility, they employ creative strategies to respond to the fact that "there aren't words for what [they] do or how [they] feel, so [they] have to make them up."[19] Often the capacity for identity construction is constrained as "we come to understand ourselves in terms of the concepts that are available to us in the time and place we live in. The language around us shapes our self-identities and our understanding of sexual identity depends on the language of sexuality available to us."[20]

The default language available to individuals in Western culture is that of monogamy (or at least that of serial monogamy). Representations of love are oversaturated with images and depictions of the amorous dyad. The widespread narratives about romantic love emphasize the importance of romantic relationships in Western culture. These love narratives uphold monogamy in positions of hegemonic dominance, as "the stories of love and relationships told by the media constrain stories of [non-monogamous] lives since the only available language is of monogamy and infidelity."[21] Non-monogamies get placed on the fringes of discursive possibilities as a result.

Still, though, we learn important lessons about non-monogamous identity by thinking about monogamous identity—for example, how individual identity tends to flow from intimate relationship practices or beliefs. Jeffery Weeks has argued that the emergence of "gay" as an identity label in the 1970s established a pathway for social recognition—a recognition that made possible a previously inaccessible sense of community and security.[22] What lies beneath "gay" identity, however, is a social recognition of the centrality of intimate relationships in our culture. The notion of a same-sex relationship (whether sexual or romantic) plays a role in the legibility of constructing "gay" identity. In other words, the quixotic same-sex relationship (whether one is presently participating in one or not) functions as an identity-defining bond which develops between relata. It is the union (or the idealized union) that is important not only to the individual(s) themselves but also to the larger social community. If the importance of intimate relationship(s) were not a thing, cultural recognition would be obscured. And while "gay" identity does admit of variation, it is difficult to conceive of this identity without centralizing a quixotic intimate relational union of any sort. Individual recognition runs alongside cultural recognition as well. That is, the importance of the quixotic intimate relational union is also important to the individuals involved. The important point to take away here is that intimate relationships (i.e., sexual or romantic) shape how we come to understand ourselves and thereby aid a process of personal development. We see that sexual and romantic relational identities are, at their core, relationship based.

Insofar as monogamy and monogamous identity are relationship-based, understanding non-monogamy as a privation of monogamy also includes understanding non-monogamy and non-monogamous identity as based on relationships as well. If monogamy is about including intimate relationships of a certain sort, then non-monogamy, even as a privation that negates monogamy, is also oriented towards how we understand intimate relationships. Thus, non-monogamy is necessarily about how we understand relationships too. So, if it can be reasonable for a person to identify as monogamous, it should also be reasonable for a person to identify as non-monogamous as well, so far as the negation of monogamy resonates with them.

Non-monogamy, as we have seen, covers quite a wide range of relationships. As this book picks out polyamory as the paradigm of why it's okay to not be monogamous, I opt for focusing on polyamorous identity in lieu of some of its counterparts (e.g., "single", "swinger", "ethically non-monogamous") save for places where it makes sense to draw points of comparisons with these intimacies and identities. One motivation not only for choosing to identify as "polyamorous" but also for focusing our analysis of non-monogamous identities on polyamory, is that "it is a category in itself not defined in contrast to the dominant way of doing relationships."[23] Polyamory offers positive conceptual content in ways that non-monogamy does not. Polyamory is not simply the negation of monogamy but is rather the participation in multiple sexual or romantic relationships at a time, with the knowledge and consent of all parties involved. The knowledge and consent conditions of polyamory also reveal something about the belief system it relies on—namely, it assumes the possibility and permissibility of existing in more than one romantic or sexual relationship at a time. It is uncontroversial to assert that these beliefs are partially constitutive of polyamory.[24]

Another motivation can be found in differentiation and distinction. We have already shown some distinction between polyamory and polyfidelity regarding relationship openness. Further, another hallmark of polyamory is the tendency to emphasize the notion of love in simultaneous romantic relationships in ways that some other non-monogamies, such as swinging, do not. Polyamorists understand themselves to have unique relational experiences that are distinct from the polyfidel and the swinger. The label "polyamorous" creates room for self-understanding and self-definition with more nuance than the label "non-monogamous" does. Importantly though, both of these motivations for constructing polyamorous identity quixotically center romantic relationships, albeit in ways different than other sexual or romantic identities. If the centrality of intimate sexual relationships can have the encompassing effect of shaping one's experiences in ways that resonate with them so much that they identify with a descriptive label that includes those experiences, it is reasonable to expect the possibility for romantic relationality to do the same. In describing a person's orientation toward intimate relationships (i.e., romantic relationships), the "polyamorous" label, then, functions as an organizing principle for persons who share a certain value set and experiences which emanate from that value set.

Polyamorous identities are socio-culturally constructed through resonances and could fall along various points of the non/monogamy spectrum. The extent to which the conventional beliefs constitutive of polyamory resonate with a person tells us about how deeply embedded a polyamorous identity is. Of course, this presupposes the possibility of a socio-culturally constructed polyamorous identity being embedded at all.

A compelling reason for thinking this is the assumption that, as agents, we have the capacity for self-naming and forging our own distinctive subject positionalities. We have already seen the extent to which individual identity can come from the importance placed on intimate romantic relationships. And while according to Tweedy, many self-identifying polyamorists are "resistant to the idea that poly-amory is an essential identity,"[25] polyamorous scholars have referred to the capacity for self-naming and identifying as polyamorous as an existential right.[26] This is consistent with experiences of self-identifying polyamorists who report "understanding, from an early age, that they wanted types of relationships that differed from the societal norm."[27] If Rambukkana is right, then compromising someone's capacity for doing this constitutes a kind of moral harm. More than this, if societies, states, and governments have some hand in this compromise, then they fall short of justice. For example, might people be more reluctant to identify as "polyamorous" if they are already living under oppressive regimes such as amatonormativity, heteronormativity, and mononormativity? Might people of color be more reluctant to identify as "poly-amorous" if they are already living not only under these regimes but also racism and white supremacy?

I maintain with Tweedy, Emens, Rambukkana, and others that polyamorous identity is a socially constructed one. Specifically, it is a socially constructed identity having to do with a particular set of values and beliefs—namely, that it is possible and permissible to exist in multiple romantic or sexual relationships at the same time with the knowledge and consent of the parties involved. By stating that non-monogamous identities are "not, strictly speaking, identities", I mean simply that they are not essential identities and as such contain the potential for mutability.

SUMMARY

Sometimes, monogamy is used in ways that suggest deviations from the social convention as outlined in Chapter 1. For example, sometimes people who engage in non-monogamous relating whether ethically (i.e., permissible extrarelational sex) or unethically (i.e., cheating) still identify as monogamous. While monogamy is not, straightforwardly speaking an identity, I presented an account of identity that is rooted in a notion of embeddedness of belief. I modified this account to include resonances. Taken together, the account of romantic relational identity as embeddedness provides a pathway for understanding the association between monogamy and monogamous identity (so-to-speak). Namely, the extent that tenants of monogamy resonate with someone tells us which of those beliefs are embedded within that person. Generally speaking, the more deeply these monogamous tenants resonate, the more likely a person would be to adopt monogamy as an identity.

The composite account of embeddedness is mutable and contains real possibilities for changes to one's identity. When these shifts happen, embeddedness can explain how and why the shift took place; as one finds a system of belief more dissonant than resonant (even if it were true that what is now dissonant was, at one time, deeply resonant), we could reasonably expect the identity category to be repudiated by the person. How likely these shifts are or how often they take place, are both empirical questions beyond the scope of current inquiry.

The embeddedness account understands monogamy as being wide enough in scope to accommodate singles, unmarried couples that are in marriage-like relationships, and a range of seemingly non-monogamous involvements such as cheating or having threesomes. Importantly, it is also wide enough to accommodate non-monogamous identities such as "swingers" or "polyamorists". Because non-monogamy covers such a wide range of intimacies, it does not offer any positive content, making it a deflationary option for identifying or forging distinctive subjective positionalities. In the section on non-monogamous identities, I looked at polyamorous identity as a kind of non-monogamous identity. As a kind of romantic relational identity, polyamorous identities are socially constructed similar to the ways monogamous ones are.

REFERENCES

Brake, Elizabeth. *Minimizing Marriage: Marriage, morality, and the law*. Oxford University Press, 2012.

Clardy, Justin Leonard. "Toward a progressive black sexual politics: reading African American Polyamorous Women in Patricia Hill Collins' Black Feminist Thought." In *The Routledge Companion to Romantic Love*, pp. 153–161. Routledge, 2021.

Clardy, Justin Leonard. "'I don't want to be a playa no more': an exploration of the denigrating effects of 'player' as a stereotype against African

American Polyamorous Men." *AnALize: Revista de studii feminist* 11 (25) (2018): 38–60.

Emens, Elizabeth F. "Monogamy's law: compulsory monogamy and polyamorous existence." *NYU Review of Law & Social Change* 29 (2004): 277.

Jenkins, Carrie. *What Love Is: and what it could be.* Basic Books, 2017.

Macrosson, Samuel A. "Constructive immutability." *University of Pennsylvania. Journal of Constitutional Law* 3 (2001): 646.

Rambukkana, Nathan Patrick. "Uncomfortable bridges: The bisexual politics of outing polyamory," *Journal of Bisexuality* 4, no. 3–4 (2004): 141–154.

Rickert, Eve, and Carrie Jenkins, "Canada defines love—exclusively (with Carrie Jenkins)." *Medium*, October 31, 2020, https://everickert.medium. com/canada-defines-love-exclusively-63bd57e4ac3d.

Ritchie, Ani, and Meg Barker. "'There aren't words for what we do or how we feel so we have to make them up': Constructing polyamorous languages in a culture of compulsory monogamy." *Sexualities* 9, no. 5 (2006): 584–601.

Tweedy, Ann E. "Polyamory as a sexual orientation." *University of Cincinnati Law Review* 79 (2010): 1461.

Weeks, Jeffrey. *Sexuality.* Routledge, 2003.

Witte Jr, John. *The Western Case for Monogamy Over Polygamy.* Cambridge University Press, 2015.

Four

INTRODUCTION

Throughout this book, I have maintained that intimate relationships do not exist in a vacuum. Instead, personal intimate relationships exist in a wider context of structural inequalities that enhance or stifle the pursuit of a flourishing life. This chapter leaves discussions that surround polyamory's standing as ethically permissible for Chapters 1 through 3. The present chapter attempts to move beyond discussions of the ethicality of polyamories and situate polyamorous people and their relationships in the broader political landscape.

Interest in polyamory has been increasing in both the public and the media. It is estimated that more and more people are hearing about (and participating in) non-monogamies than ever before. Apryl Alexander's research reports that roughly 60% of Americans have heard of the term 'polyamory' via mass media and that between 4–5% of the U.S. population are currently involved in a consensually non-monogamous relationship. She reports on surveys of American singles as well, where 21% of the participants say that they've been in an "open sexual relationship".[1] Furthermore, in 2010 Deborah Anapol found that roughly one out of every 500 adults in the United States is polyamorous.[2]

DOI: 10.4324/9781003375036-5

In America, polyamorous relationships have been an increasing site of political activity. Den Otter notes that several developed countries are moving in the direction of decriminalizing polygamy and legally protecting multiperson intimate relationships.[3] In 2020, the U.S. city of Sommerville, Massachusetts, extended rights to polyamorous relationships that were historically reserved for spouses in a marriage. In the same year, amidst a public health crisis and global pandemic, Marco Mendicino (Canada's Minister of Immigration, Refugees, and Citizenship) "announced that unmarried romantic partners of Canadians would be allowed to cross the border" to see their romantic partners.[4] However, Canada's official definition of eligible relationships included the requirement that those relationships are "exclusive" (read as monogamous). Whether we admit it or not, our romantic relationships are always part of a larger social and political context. As examples like these show, prompting questions about the political consequences and impact on polyamorous relationships is urgent.

In liberal societies, it is reasonable to expect that people will have different views on what makes life worthwhile. It is uncontroversial that in a liberal society, without compelling reasons not to do so, people should be able to think and act how they please in the pursuit of their flourishing. In the U.S., these life chances are complicated by the supervenience of legal, political, and normative pressures upon people's desires. Critics of marriage and monogamy have taken stock of these complications. For example, in the 1970s and 1980s, some feminist critiques aimed at marriage as an essentially patriarchal institution, the role of "coupling" in upholding capitalism, entitlement and possessiveness, and hierarchies.

Since the turn of the millennium, legal theorists have been asking questions like how does the institution of marriage factor into polyamorous marginalization, exclusion, and violence? Are polyamorists a political group worthy of special protections under the law? And, broadly speaking, what might justice for polyamorists look like?

Just as our intimate relational practices are a fine subject for ethical scrutiny, so too might a society's systems, institutions, and laws be brought under the microscope. Governments and laws can be good or bad; right or wrong; fair or unfair; harmful or helpful. In the U.S., marriage has perhaps the most prominent role in policing the intimate lives of its subjects. According to Elizabeth Brake, 1,138 federal statutory provisions consider marital status as a factor in determining benefits, rights, and privileges.[5] This has led some scholars down the long-trodden road of marriage disestablishment and others down the road of more subtle marriage reform measures they believe get us closer to justice for all.

In the first section of this chapter, relying on the conception of liberal neutrality, I make clear what a liberal state's responsibilities are to its subjects whose intimate relational practices deviate from the mononormative standard. In the second section, I look at similarities between the marriage equality struggle advanced by proponents of same-sex marriage and arguments for extending marriage rights to multi-party unions. In the final section of the chapter, I treat some objections to the extension of marriage rights to multi-party unions. Ultimately, I argue that societies that care about treating their subjects fairly must take the possibility that marriage should not be restricted to monogamous dyads seriously.

POLITICAL LIBERALISM AND WHAT IT REQUIRES OF MARRIAGE

John Rawls is one of the most influential political philosophers in the history of political liberalism and liberal thought. Rawls' lasting contributions include his understanding of public reason and liberal neutrality. Rawlsian liberalism can be contrasted with moral legalism and liberal perfectionism. Liberal perfectionists, such as Joseph Raz,[6] maintain that a society's laws should be framed in a way that responds to judgements about which human goods are worthwhile for its members to have. This view is consistent with pluralism insofar as there is a range of choices that are judged valuable. Legal moralists, such as Patrick Devlin,[7] on the other hand, maintain that to preserve society, the state should legally protect that society's moral norms. For these thinkers, this is the most effective way for a society to prevent its disintegration due to changing social mores. For Rawls, in liberal states, it should not be the case that laws and policies are drawn from religious doctrines or comprehensive moral views. The problems with legal moralism and liberal perfectionism are that, in one way or another, they endorse norms that are so drawn.

Contemporary liberal societies are characterized by a pluralism of practices (including its members' religious and moral commitments). On the Rawlsian picture, liberalism emerges from needing a resolution that accommodates competing religious commitments; he extends this further to cover competing moral doctrines as well. Importantly, Rawls is concerned with the *framing* of laws and not their *effects*. The contours of how just laws and institutions must be framed are contained within the limits of *public reason* and *liberal neutrality*.

He says, "The idea of public reason specifies at the deepest level the basic moral and political values that are to determine a constitutional democratic government's relation to its citizens and their relation to one another."[8] In her concentration on marriage law, Brake recounts the requirements of Rawls' idea of public reason saying:

> public reason requires that in deciding public matters, especially 'matters of fundamental justice,' and in the political sphere (the courts and the legislature), citizens must give reasons which they could reasonably expect those with different conceptions of the good drawn from different comprehensive moral, philosophical, or religious doctrines to accept.[9]

Public reasons are reasons offered, that we can reasonably expect members of even a diverse and pluralistic society, to accept; and they do not depend on moral, philosophical, or religious doctrines. Public reasons are thus narrowly defined—they concern the political, primarily.

While public reason situates one of the constraints on the framing of public policies and institutions, liberal neutrality situates the other. Similar to public reasons, liberal neutrality also prohibits conceptions of the good that are drawn from comprehensive moral or religious doctrines. In *Political Liberalism*, Rawls states that "basic institutions and public policy...are neutral in the sense that they can be endorsed by citizens generally as within the scope of a public political conception" and that "the state is not to do anything intended to favor or promote any particular comprehensive doctrine rather than another, or give greater assistance to those who pursue it."[10] In short, in liberal societies, there must not only be a separation of church and state but also a separation between the state and comprehensive moral doctrines as well.

There are a couple of questions that we could ask here. First, we could ask whether a just liberal society includes the institution of marriage—monogamous or otherwise. Several feminists have asked whether the promotion of coupledom protects or detracts from "the common good". For these feminists, marriage is a central factor in causing inequality and division.[11] Simon Câbuela May argues that a liberal society can, in good conscience, support a marriage institution without violating liberal neutrality because it provides instrumental reasons surrounding the "presumptive permanence" of relationships.[12] I tend to agree with May that marriage provides instrumental reasons that the state can get behind, but this is not the most relevant point. Work in non-ideal political theory starts with the world we currently have and asks how might that world be made more consistent with justice. The first question might better serve us if we were asking how a society in a pre-social state, should be set up to begin with—that is, in a society that does not yet have any institutions whatsoever, let alone an institution of marriage. I am more inclined to agree with Brake's non-ideal approach which mentions that contemporary liberal societies, already complete with legal marriage, have been distributive sites of inalienable rights. It's better to ask how this institution, if it's not inherently oppressive, can be reshaped to meet the demands of justice.

The second question takes for granted the existence of marriage. It asks whether marriage is the kind of institution that appropriately falls under the scope of constraints public reason and liberal neutrality provide. Since it does, it must be justified with public reasons because the state has a legitimate interest in marriage; marriage is a part of family formation and families are a part of the basic structure of a society.[13] Public reason and liberal neutrality require that marriage law be defined on considerations that we could reasonably expect those with different conceptions of the good to accept. Yet, as Rawls himself takes note of, "appeals to monogamy as such, or against same-sex marriages…would reflect religious or comprehensive moral doctrines."[14] These appeals, when they find their basis in moral or religious doctrines, are inappropriate and do not belong in the public arena as they do not offer public reasons and therefore violate liberal neutrality.

Some might think, like Peter de Marneffe, that monogamous marriage is justifiable through the narrow kinds of political reasons that Rawlsian liberalism requires (such as children's welfare).[15] Arguing that the state violates individual rights by criminalizing polygamous cohabitation, de Marneffe still thinks that an informed person, who takes individual rights seriously, can consistently believe that although polygamous cohabitation should be decriminalized, polygamy should not be legalized. His position goes further and maintains that it's also consistent to believe that although the government should recognize monogamous marriage as a legal status, it should not recognize a legal status for polygamy. de Marneffe believes that monogamous marriages provide a unique kind of human good that may make a person's life go better for them in ways that other kinds of relationships do not duplicate or replace without loss. He writes, "By recognizing monogamous marriage as a legal status, the government promotes valuable relationships of this kind, whereas legalizing polygamy would not have this effect."[16]

One wonders whether this view asks the right questions. de Marneffe juxtaposes polygamy and monogamous marriage, although one needn't do this. The legalization of polygamous marriage needn't come at the expense of monogamous marriage as the state may simultaneously recognize both forms. Thus, the question is not about whether or not monogamy is distinctive in its purported value, but rather if it is so *exclusively*. Care ethicists have argued that friendships and polyamorous relationships are also intimate relationships that have distinctive kinds of value and that these relationships of care ought to have the same kinds of protections as monogamous dyads under marriage. It is not inconsistent to believe that if the state is going to recognize civil marriage at all, it has a responsibility to extend the rights contained therein to multi-party unions like polyamorous relationships. If the state fails to recognize this responsibility, it risks the superimposition of a comprehensive moral or religious doctrine. The state would thereby incur the cost of harming its members (via coercive taxation, for one example) who do not share a particularly contested moral or religious view around marriage. Justly framed institutions must be justifiable through public reason and liberal neutrality and it is far from clear that monogamous marriage achieves this.

Arguments about the distinctiveness of value are in some ways akin to arguments that were offered in opposition to same-sex marriages in the early aughts (2000s). It was thought, for example, that different-sex unions were distinctively valuable given their "reproductive complimentarality". Liberals have notably used rationales consistent with Rawlsian thinking to justify their arguments for same-sex marriage. To date, these rationales offer compelling reasons for accepting the proposition that a liberal state has compelling reasons justifiable through public reason and liberal neutrality for extending marriage rights, privileges, and protections to multi-party unions. Brake has urged that

Liberal defenses of same-sex marriage have not followed the implications of their reasoning far enough. Attempts within liberalism to produce a rationale for restricting legal marriage to different-sex partners have failed, but so have attempts to produce a rationale for restricting it to monogamous or amatonormative relationships.[17]

Brake points out that the current institution of American marriage wrongly discriminates across intimate personal relationships based on amatonormative assumptions. I add that it does so based on mononormative ones as well. While there is significant overlap and interplay between these concepts, we should understand that marriage can at once be amatonormative and not mononormative. Brake stresses the extent to which amatonormativity picks out "amorous, enduring, central love relationship(s)" and in other places, she stresses that amatonormativity also covers "marriage" and "marriage-like" relationships. While she realizes that in the current political landscape marriage and marriage-like relationships are dyadic, notice though that the concept of amatonormativity does not make explicit reference to a number of relata. Thus, in some possible world where plural marriages are legal, polyfidels might marry in non-dyadic ways and still prioritize and centralize their multiple love relationships (i.e., their marriage(s)) precisely because they are amorous and enduring. If in this possible world marriage is still wrongly discriminatory against, say, friendships, and incentivizes marriage relationships at their expense, this world would still unquestionably be amatonormative.

In our actual world, plural marriages are not legal and are instead criminalized.[18] Marriage is mononormative insofar as, structurally, the only intimate relationships that stand under its protection are dyadic. Culturally, marriages are thought to be essentially monogamous without question or criticism. Many people still believe there to be some superiority in nuclear family structures and exclusive romantic relationships to provide value that is itself both distinctive and exclusively so. As we saw in an earlier chapter, however, the jury is far from settled on questions about whether non-monogamous parenting dynamics are on the whole detrimental to children. We have also seen the ways that polyamorous relationships and friendships may be ethically advantageous, and thereby valuable, for relata. Both in our actual world and the possible world sketched above, amatonormative and mononormative discriminations made on the basis that these marriage and marriage-like relationships are *more valuable* than other intimate relationship forms are wrong. Currently, monogamous marriage fails to satisfy public reason and liberal neutrality, so, the discriminations it makes regarding personal intimate relationships is unjust because it rests on illegitimate premises.

In its current form, marriage propagates mononormativity and amatonormativity at the expense of polyamorists, friends, and other non-monogamists. It marginalizes these groups by offering protections only to amorous dyadic relationships. The association with the more well-known normative pressure of heteronormativity has a lengthy history in marriage's legacy. Heteronormativity, which refers to the assumption of heterosexuality and gender as prescriptive norms, was a primary aim of many critiques of marriage from feminists and LBGTQ+ activists alike in the marriage equality movement in the United States before *Obergefell v. Hodges* in 2015 which struck down bans on same-sex marriage nationwide. A central claim of those arguments is that a marriage institution that protects and legitimizes only different-sex relationships endorses a view of relationships that do not offer legitimate public reasons and therefore violates what liberal neutrality requires of liberal states.

While marriage rights activists have issued claims, and rightfully so, that beliefs around reproductive complimentarity reflects commitments to comprehensive moral or religious values (i.e., that a primary purpose of marriage is reproductive sex), they have not as eagerly advanced arguments for forms of plural marriage. This is surprising given that the two (i.e., same-sex marriage and plural marriage) have been straightforwardly linked in political discourse. For example, Elizabeth Emens recounts political conservative Rick Santorum's 2003 statement that "'[I]f the Supreme Court says that you have the right to consensual (gay) sex within your home then you have the right to bigamy, you have the right to polygamy, you have the right to incest, you have the right to adultery. You have the right to anything.'"[19] Santorum was motivated by the worry that same-sex marriage would eventually lead to "abominable" practices such as polygamy. Ronald den Otter maintains that we cannot avoid extending those rationales offered in favor of same-sex marriage to plural and multi-party marriage. It is to those considerations that I now turn.

PLURAL MARRIAGES

Discrimination against non-monogamous relationships (and their practitioners) and the possibility of plural marriage (and its enthusiasts) is wrong precisely because it rests on false assumptions about the value monogamous intimate relationships have. Proponents of same-sex marriage and plural marriage alike have argued that marital status mediates how benefits such as inheritance rights, tax and immigration status, and other legal protections are allocated. Although there is a slim philosophical tradition apparent within the history of philosophy (for example, David Hume, Immanuel Kant, Hegel, John Stuart Mill, and W.E.B. Du Bois can all be spotted remarking on plural marriages in their thought), I am of the view that the most enlightening insights into polyamory and the impacts on its practitioners since the turn of the millennium have come from legal theory. It is from legal theorists that we learn that a principle legal function of marriage is to adjudicate third-party benefits claims, for example.[20] Work from legal scholars is a promising site for our philosophical thinking about how marriage can be made more just for non-monogamists.

Despite the power that states in the U.S. have to expand its definition of marriage to include multiple persons without acting unconstitutionally, the United States Supreme Court has not tried a case on plural marriage since the nineteenth century. Nathan Rambukkana talks about how the relationship between Canada's earliest antipolygamy laws (first appearing in Canada in 1892) was tethered to United States antipolygamy policies established 30 years prior in 1862.[21] On July 2nd, 1892, Abraham Lincoln signed the Morrill Anti-Bigamy Act, which banned bigamy in federal territories. Recently, Den Otter has argued that the United States cannot rule out a *constitutional right* to plural marriage. While skepticism about the recognition of a constitutional right to plural marriage may be well founded, skeptics should be reminded that there was comparable skepticism around the legitimization of same-sex marriage before 2015. To my mind, this suggests that we'd do well to resist making definitive predictions about the possibilities of the constitutional future.

My reasons for this are not only as Brake and den Otter, but also others like Darlene Goring, Elizabeth Emens, and Ann Tweedy point out, marriage has always been a highly variable institution.[22] Quoting Sanford Levinson, Den Otter writes, "It is always the case that courts are perpetually open to a new argument about rights…that reflect the dominant public opinion of the day."[23] Presently, the meaning of marriage is evolving in some local governments. In 2020, two Massachusetts cities, Sommerville and Cambridge, have taken steps in this direction. Both cities have redefined "domestic partnerships" to include relationships involving more than two people, extending to them the same rights as married couples. Still, civil unions are not substitutions for marriages.

Some of the reasons that have been offered for same-sex marriage, such as those having to do with public reasons and liberal neutrality, are just as compelling for considering the extension of marriage rights to multi-party unions. It is remarkable that the growing tolerance of sexual minorities that lead many Americans to reject the view that marriage has to be between a man and a woman, has not yet led to a majority view that people should be allowed to marry more than one person at a time. Den Otter posits that in the minds of many Americans, "a numerical limitation differs significantly from one based on sexual orientation and is consequently much easier to defend…For some of them it is obvious that the constitutional right of marriage cannot be extended beyond couples."[24] Unless marriage changes to become more accommodating to multi-party unions, the normative pressures applied by mononormativity and amatonormativity will thus continue to have costly impacts on polyamorists and other non-monogamies including tax status, criminal liability, legal disadvantages regarding child custody,[25] and even in immigration matters.[26]

Some philosophers have treated the global and national shifts in public opinion and political landscape as an occasion to examine further positive reforms. Treating successful philosophical arguments for same-sex marriage as their starting point, the comparisons between rationales offered have prompted questions by liberal political theorists about which relationships, if any at all, should the state promote and why. Does marriage reform go far enough in the direction of liberalism? Should the institution of marriage be abolished altogether?

Den Otter calls out the state's hypocrisy. Despite what he calls a "checkered past" (including positive correlations with the subordination of women, intimate partner violence, child abuse and neglect, or other sociopathic behaviors) with different or same-sex monogamy there are only a few contemporary scholars who maintain that we should abolish traditional marriage or that it should be disestablished altogether. His argument, however, is that when a legal system in a liberal society does not make room for plural marriage, it compromises the liberty of those who are denied the option of marrying the person(s) of their choice. Harm is thereby issued at the hand of the state—particularly, polyamorists and other non-monogamies "may not be able to have as good a life as they could have had or achieve their most important ends."[27] Fundamentally, then, the state has a responsibility to consider "whether a restriction on the right to choose a partner is sufficiently justified to override the normally strong presumption in favor of letting adults make their own decisions about the way they want to live."[28] While den

Otter's argument thoroughly examines the constitutionality of plural marriage arguing that America's well-established constitutional tradition supports the expansion of marriage to multi-party unions based on individual liberty, some scholars have opted to go the route of invoking a principle of equal treatment and arguing that the state's arbitrary exclusions of multi-party unions, like polyamorists, violate this principle.

Tweedy critically points out that much of the question about the extensions of rights for polyamorists as such, turns on whether or not polyamorists even desire legal protections at all, let alone the ones that marriage provides. Some are of the mind that a language and agenda that centralize the importance of "rights" for polyamorists might compromise the potentiality for polyamory to occupy a more radical queer subject position and thereby, it is a less radical transformative politic.[29] Additionally, Hadar Aviram's ethnographic study of Bay Area polyamorous activists highlights polyamorists' reluctance to seek legal changes through the thoughtful rejections of certain kinds of political motives.[30] In other places, however, polyamorists have spoken up about the importance of securing political protections around employment harassment and discrimination.[31] In 1996, a political quiz with more than 200 respondents showed 68% of polyamorists favored civil group marriage with 32% opposing it.[32] Furthermore the recent shifts in local governments of Sommerville and Cambridge Massachusetts, respectively reflect an increase in an expressed desire for the protection of civil marriages. In 2021, three polyamorous men in California fought (and won) to have their polyamorous relationship recognized by having all of their names included on their child's birth certificate.[33] Thus the political landscape among polyamorists is diverse and it reveals that polyamorists are not, at current, a monolith.

Understandably, some polyamorists desire to be treated as legal equals under civil marriage. Den Otter states that "they… want to be treated as legal equals because they do not want the state to act as an ethical authority that marginalizes their intimate relationships and in doing so, diminishes their lives."[34] Among those polyamorists that do urge political mobilization, some of their arguments from equal treatment have appealed to anti-discrimination laws. Den Otter goes on to say:

> When one is asking for the right to marry more than one person simultaneously, he or she is not only asking for the state to treat the marital relationship he or she wants to form equally. He or she is also requesting that the state respect his or her freedom of choice to let him or her be the judge of who his or her partner is going to be— perhaps for the rest of his or her life. The failure to permit plural marriage would deny that choice to someone who is already married to only one person, and it would also deny that choice to those who are not already married as to their first choice of marital partner.[35]

Importantly, much of the legal success in bringing anti-discrimination claims forward has depended on the ability of a given class to do two things: (1) To show themselves as an actual class or group and (2) then to be able to analogize their situation to that of other oppressed groups. Ann Tweedy goes some way in establishing a conceptual basis for thinking about polyamory as a kind of relational identity and indeed one that faces considerable discrimination and deserves the protected status of other marginalized classes or groups. There is also evidence that polyamorists' self-conception includes understanding themselves as a kind of minority group as Emens has shown "polys recognize that only a minority of people seek honest, open, and autonomous non-monogamy in the ways that polys do."[36] Because of the ways that amatonormativity and mononormativity unduly discriminate against non-monogamies, "non-monogamy is an organizing principle of inequality in American culture"[37] that must be rejected.

RECOGNIZING NON-MONOGAMIES AND SOME CONCOMITANT CHALLENGES

In this section, I wish to focus on Elizabeth Brake's work because it presents one of the more compelling sketches of what is required of marriage in a liberal society. In another context, one that aims at abolishing the prison industrial complex, Allegra McLeod follows a tradition that can be attributed to thinkers like Angela Davis[38] and argues that proposed reforms to social and political institutions that are "unfinished" contain a source of critical strength and possibilities as they seek to confront legislative state harm. On her view, unfinished alternatives provide a "sketch" of how existing states of affairs can be changed through interventions that are partial, incomplete, and in process.[39] While institutional reforms must be cautious of relying on mechanisms that may sustain problematic political forces, they must be articulated in terms that are recognizable and conceivable to those who exist in the current state of affairs. So, reforms should thus be both unlike the current state of affairs and simultaneously legible within them because the public imaginary is in many ways constrained by the status quo. I read Brake's proposals for marriage reform, or what she terms "minimal marriage", informed by McLeod's insights. That is, I read minimal marriage as a set of unfinished alternatives that invite input from members of the society that are subject to having their intimate lives unjustly discriminated against. Both, as I present Brake's account and after, I respond to some concerns about plural marriage.

Brake's inquiry is guided by the thought that supporting caring relationships is an important matter of justice. One of Brake's central claims is that "if caring relationships are a good whose support is a matter of justice, such relationships deserve support in all their forms"[40] and so friendship and other non-traditional partnerships such as polyamories[41] deserve marriage entitlements. She views polyamory as the "best-case scenario" for group marriage rights.[42] and calls her agenda for marriage reform "minimal marriage". On her account, minimal marriage is not only consistent with liberalism (and indeed it is for her as it is justifiable within public reason) but it is required by a liberal state to provide such a framework for personal relationships. Liberal principles require a radical restructuring of marriage that recognizes the many forms of caring relationships.

Forgoing reasons of state stability, the satisfaction of citizens' preferences, and the recognition of autonomy, she opts for a uniquely neutral rationale for minimal marriage. For Brake, caring relationships are primary goods and the social bases that make them possible are social primary goods. A key difference between a "primary good" and a "social primary good" has to do with the distributive power that a state has. She compares caring relationships to the primary good of self-respect saying that neither are appropriate bases for interpersonal comparisons and that the state cannot distribute these goods directly. The social basis—i.e., the rights that she takes to be associated with minimal marriage that would support, recognize, and protect them—of these relationships are subject to state distribution. Caring relationships fall within the purview of primary goods because they are an essential site where moral agency is cultivated and exercised. They are all-purpose means normally needed in the pursuit of pluralistic conceptions of the good.

A primary tenet of minimal marriage is the idea "that individuals can have legal marital relationships with more than one person, reciprocally or asymmetrically, themselves determining the sex and number of parties, the type of relationship involved, and which rights and responsibilities to exchange with each."[43] Brake states, "Minimal marriage allows individuals to select from the rights and responsibilities exchanged within marriage and exchange them with whomever they want, rather than exchanging a predefined bundle of rights and responsibilities with only one amatory partner."[44] Ultimately, the framework for minimal marriage has fewer state-determined restrictions than does the institution's present form. Still, Brake believes that "minimal marriage institutes the most extensive set of restrictions on marriage compatible with political liberalism."[45] The rights associated with minimal marriage cannot be specified outside of their social context, but she lists some rights that are apt candidates in an ideal egalitarian society including, "eligibility for spousal immigration, employment and relocation assistance, and preferential hiring (currently offered to U.S. military and civil service spouses and by some private employers), residency (where relevant for in-state tuition, etc.), ... status designation for the purpose of third parties offering other benefits (such as employment incentives or family rates)"[46] and a few others.[47]

Importantly, the rights reserved for minimal marriage are disaggregated as this marks a key difference and divergence from the aggregated collection of rights (all of which are exchanged at once) under contemporary civil marriage. Brake's minimal marriage does not require that parties to the marriage exchange marriage rights reciprocally or in complete bundles. Alongside the possibility of exchanging all of one's marital rights reciprocally with one other person, this creates the possibility of marital rights being distributed across the variety of relationships polyamorists have as well.

When it comes to considering whether or not polyamorists are apt candidates for the kind of pluralistic marriage that minimal marriage is, some challenges do emerge. Are polyamorous relationships sufficiently prevalent to demand legislative attention? Are polyamorists a distinctive class of individuals that can lay claim to equal treatment? Is polyamory unstable and therefore legislatively infeasible? Do polyamorous marriage rights devalue same-sex marriage rights in the ways that some polyamorists seem to think it does? We have already addressed some of these challenges such as whether or not polyamory is a stable intimate relationship that can provide a stable family unit. We've also addressed inegalitarianism and polyamory.

Regarding the prevalence of polyamory and its distinctiveness for class protection, we might question whether the standard being set is a reasonable one. Writers maintain that there is not yet much academic research on polyamorists. Furthermore, Brake writes that these questions emerge from a rationale that "sets an impossible standard for legal reform, as research cannot be carried out...until reform has taken place."[48]

Also, existing in a society that does not already provide the legal support for such relationships, familiar problematics of "passing" and "closeting" emerge. Noting that "polyamorists can hide their non-traditional relationships more easily than gays and lesbians," they are incentivized to do so as they face social and legal penalties for living their lifestyles openly.[49] According to Brake, in amatonormative and mononormative societies like the U.S., these penalties include the threat of children being removed from polyamorous families, job discrimination, and social stigma. Whatever the number of polyamorists presently reported, the convergence of these social pressures likely conceals larger numbers. As a result, the argument that the percentage of polyamorists is tiny and therefore is not deserving of anti-discrimination attention, loses some of its teeth. Elanor Wilkinson writes that an important part of political movements surrounding marginalized sexualities is a move toward greater public visibility leading to recognition, tolerance and acceptance.[50] The importance of polyamorous representation, therefore, in art and mass media cannot be understated. This aligns with arguments of political motivation that require a particular kind of attentiveness to the situational vulnerabilities of marginalized groups.[51]

Since minimal marriages propose a disaggregation of marital rights and privileges some might think that "difficulties arise with extending marital privilege…to groups."[52] In other words, the structure that minimal marriage proposes is unnecessarily complicated. Wouldn't opening the door to group relationships open the door for fraudulent marriage claims involving inordinately large groups? Can a person extend unlimited immigration rights to as many spouses as they'd like? And how might that affect domestic and foreign policies around immigration and citizenship? We can meet these objections by pointing out that minimal marriage is not some kind of free-for-all. As Den Otter points out, some restrictions on marriage would be obvious such as ones about age, competence, and species as they lack the ability to consent. Also, we might reasonably assume that at a certain point, some dynamics might be so large as to be unattractive to polyamorists.

Brake mentions that under minimal marriage we should be reminded that some of the rights are of little cost to the state (e.g., caretaking leave) and thus have little incentive to abuse via fraudulence. There is also an important link between immigration law and limits on number. Presently immigration eligibility for spouses is already investigated by the state requiring spouses to demonstrate that they know each other well, share a history of interaction, and stand in a non-fungible relationship with one another. For Kolodny and others, at the very least this simply just is what it means to be in a relationship with someone. On one hand, if it can be shown that inordinately large groups bear this kind of connection to one another, then there is no principled reason under minimal marriage for their marriage to be ruled out. This principle is fine to stand on. It is especially strong if we are to, as Brake does, appeal to research about the psychological limits to the number of relationships that we can sustain.[53] A society where a thoroughgoing demonstration of caring relationships is not required should also be conceivable too. In contemporary mononormative societies, dyadic couples can marry for a range of reasons. Dyadic couples marry for reasons that could be trivial but still sufficient for marriage including wanting a trophy wife, to avoid embarrassment or shame due to having premarital sex that led to an unwanted pregnancy, to form political allegiances to run for public office, or to never have to shop for one's clothes again. These motives however are seldom (if ever) probed in the case of dyadic marriage.

Finally, we'd do well to address residual worries about polyamory and inequality. Some concerns about equality and polyamory, as we have already noted, have to do with gendered power imbalances. The thought here is that the state's permitting plural marriage via minimal marriage may cause or contribute to gender inequality. If this is true, one may object that the state has interests in not promoting gender inequality and stopping the coercion of women. Others have to do with legislative inequalities having to deal with things like property and divorce. What happens if A, B, and C marry and after some time B and C divorce with alimony being due from B to C? Minimal marriage might entitle C to A's assets under A's marriage to B. Also, if marriage is left to be legislated at the state level, polyamorous spouses might still face inequality in how they are governed across state lines. Den Otter puts the point quite simply, "any state that allow[s] a person to marry more than one person simultaneously within its borders would have raised the question of whether other states that do not perform such marriages must treat them as legally valid when a multi-person intimate union visits or becomes residents."[54]

Regarding the concern about potential gendered imbalances, it might be that "multiple wives will be better off if they have legal marital rights; legal marriage rights for multiple spouses might actually discourage male-headed polygyny rather than embracing it."[55] Additionally, some empirical work on polyamory claims that women are on the whole more comfortable with relating non-monogamously than men are. These considerations are worth taking into account before rushing to the judgment that plural marriage under a minimal marriage framework would inevitably lead to a kind of polygamy that is dominated by polygynous folks.

The aforementioned problem of assets emerges from conceiving of marital rights as necessarily exclusive and transitive. The thought is that A would lose assets or entitlements when B transfers these assets or entitlements to C. Speaking to the problem of inequality and assets, Brake argues that rights can be specified so that they are not transitive. For instance, it could be that, as both Emens and Brake explore, the law implements minimal marriage using a form listing the prospective entitlements (and their numerical limits). "Spouses could tick off boxes to indicate the rights they chose to transfer to another person or persons."[56] Emens advances that instead of using criminal law to compel relational choices, the state should encourage parties to make express agreements about how their relationship will be governed without expressing condemnation of nonexclusivity. For Brake, the implementation of marital rights in this way would require relata to learn what rights and responsibilities they are taking on precisely because of the ways that they would come to bear those rights and responsibilities. Another positive corollary is that in addition to having the choice to designate which rights would be transitive and which ones would not, this implementation of minimal marriage would allow relata to determine the reach of the state in matters of "adultery". While adultery laws are seldom enforced, more than half the states in the U.S. have laws that criminalize extramarital sex whether or not the relata consent to non-monogamy. She suggests that statutes criminalizing adultery be rewritten to reflect the choices that members of a liberal society should have. For example, a marriage form could treat non-monogamous relationships as a kind of default while providing the options for participants to either opt-in to exclusive relationships if they so choose. Thus, minimal marriage also has potential for disrupting how we think about adultery and criminality.

SUMMARY

The resistance to plural marriage in the United States reaches back to the nineteenth century and has been tied to political controversies. Many people still resist plural marriage because they believe it evidences a free-for-all with no logical stopping point. However, the country's demographic is now shifting with 4%-5% of Americans claiming they are polyamorous. Yet, by and large, the state does not recognize, protect, or otherwise provide the social bases for these polyamorous relationships. The lived reality of polyamorists includes the loss of jobs due to discrimination based on their relationships and having their possibilities for family planning impacted by zoning laws that contain numerical restrictions on unrelated persons living in the same home.[57] Even though courts are perpetually open to hearing new arguments about rights, no statutes or principles have been raised to protect them from these kinds of discriminations.

Throughout this chapter, I have maintained, with Brake that polyamorous relationships need support and protection that the state is uniquely able to provide and is best placed to carry out. Beyond the needs for support and recognition that polyamorists themselves have, a liberal society has a responsibility to provide a social basis that supports even some points of view that are presently minoritized and uniquely positioned. Just because a way of relating might deviate from well-established social norms like monogamy, this does not mean that they don't have considerable value— morally, socially, or politically. State support of only monogamous relationships under its marital institution reflects a commitment to a controversial comprehensive moral doctrine.

One such way that the state may meet its responsibility to provide a social basis for polyamorous relationships is to reform civil marriage to reflect the requirements of minimal marriage. Minimal marriage provides a philosophical justification of plural marriage under political liberalism that meets public reason and liberal neutrality. State support of monogamy reflects a commitment to a controversial comprehensive moral doctrine. Minimal marriage proposes a set of legal rights that would function as the social basis of support for polyamorous relationships.

Despite the belief that relegating plural relationships to the realm of civil unions would do polyamorists just as well as civil marriage, civil unions are not substitutes for marriages. Some might also think liberal societies do a better job of placing intimacies on equal footing by abolishing the institution of marriage altogether instead of merely "rebranding" it. I maintain that the argument for minimal marriage presented in this chapter is what some legal scholars call an "unfinished alternative" that invites feedback from the very members of society that it seeks to govern. As such, I remain open to being convinced of more radical proposals which posit that marriage abolition is what is required from a liberal state.

To date, however, I am situated in the school of thought that believes that reasons for marriage can satisfy public reason and liberal neutrality and as such preserving (but extending) the marriage institution goes some way toward rectifying past wrongs to those who amatonormativity and mononormativity has historically discriminated against based on their relational identities or relational choices. It cannot be ignored that the state has had a hand in sustaining the discrimination and penalties that reify amatonormativity and mononormativity. I also find much favor in Brake's suggestion that "such rectification might also take the form of an apology, reparations, or a monument to victims of discrimination on the basis of sexual orientation."[58]

The legal recognition of multiple forms of intimate relationships under marriage may enable the creation of new social scripts for intimate relating. Minimal marriage indeed disrupts the present meaning of marriage in ways that we can expect many to resist. However, the meaning of marriage has always been in flux and never essential. This framework creates a pathway for recognizing multi-party relationships in a way that does not indirectly foster problematic distinctions between the married and the unmarried. It does so by not intending to confer legitimacy over the relationships it covers but instead by merely conferring a status designation. Above all else, the extension of marital rights is consistent with the history of constitutional law that seeks to recognize rights under the equal protection clause of the U.S. constitution. To deny these rights and thereby equal treatment to polyamorists as such is at once harmful and unacceptable.

REFERENCES

Alexander, Apryl A. "'We Don't Do That!': Consensual Non-Monogamy in HBO's Insecure." *Journal of Black Sexuality and Relationships* 6, no. 2 (2019): 1–16.

Anapol, Deborah M. *Polyamory the new love without limits: Secrets of sustainable intimate relationships.*

Aviram, Hadar. "Geeks, goddesses, and green eggs: Political mobilization and the cultural locus of the polyamorous community in the San Francisco Bay Area." in *Understanding Non-monogamies*, ed. Meg Barker and Darren Langdridge, 99–105. New York: Routledge, 2010.

Brake, Elizabeth. "Equality and non-hierarchy in marriage: what do feminists really want?," in *After Marriage: Rethinking Marital Relationships* ed. Elizabeth Brake, 100–124. New York: Oxford University Press, 2016.

Brake, Elizabeth. *Minimizing Marriage: Marriage, morality, and the law.* Oxford University Press, 2012.

Brake, Elizabeth. "Recognizing Care: The case for friendship and polyamory." *Syracuse Journal of Law and Civic Engagement* 1, no. 1 (2015): 441.

Case, Mary Anne. "Marriage Licenses." *Minnesota Law Review* 89 (2004): 1758.

Cherry, Myisha. *The Case for Rage:Why anger is essential to anti-racist struggle.* Oxford University Press, 2021.

Clardy Justin Leonard. "Civic Tenderness as a Response to Child Poverty in America." in *Philosophy and Child Poverty* ed. Nicolás Brando and Gottfried Schweiger, 303–320. Springer Nature, 2019.

Davis, Angela Y. *Are Prisons Obsolete?* Seven Stories Press, 2011.

De Marneffe, Peter. "Liberty and Polygamy." in *After Marriage: Rethinking marital relationships* ed. Elizabeth Brake, 125–159. New York: Oxford University Press, 2016.

Den Otter, Ronald C. *In Defense of Plural Marriage.* New York: Cambridge University Press, 2015.

Devlin, Patrick. *The Enforcement of Morals.* Oxford: Oxford University Press, 1965.

Emens, Elizabeth F. "Monogamy's Law: Compulsory Monogamy and Polyamorous Existence." *NYU Review of Law & Social Change* 29 (2004): 277.

Goring, Darlene C. "The history of slave marriage in the United States." *John Marshall Law Review* 39 (2005): 299.

Karimi, Faith. "Three dads, a baby, and the legal battle to get their names added to a birth Certificate." Accessed December 31, 2021, www.cnn.com/2021/03/06/us/throuple-three-dads-and-baby-trnd/index.html

May, Simon Cãbuela. "Liberal Neutrality and Civil Marriage." in *After Marriage: Rethinking marital relationships* ed. Elizabeth Brake, 9–28. New York: Oxford University Press, 2016.

McLeod, Allegra M. "Confronting Criminal Law's Violence: The Possibilities of Unfinished Alternatives." *Harvard Unbound* 8, (2013): 109–132.

Nussbaum, Martha C. *Political Emotions*. Cambridge, MA: Harvard University Press, 2013.

Rambukkana, Nathan, and Wilfrid Laurier. "Protecting the Intimate Space of the Nation: Intimacy, Privilege and Canadian Antipolygamy Laws 1892–2012." Accessed December 30, 2021, https://d1wqtxt s1xzle7.cloudfront.net/32348223/Rambukkana_-_Protecting_ the_Intimate_Space_of_the_Nation__SSA13_Talk-with-cover-page- v2.pdf?Expires=1640918036&Signature=YlyPGpAib-uExsiwVfce bHTlFfnce1CCSHXwPQI5RTw-ta06mA-VkMMGwAl0RegCjfSjsiB i3Qe0sWDxAV-mdstG89Zgt0o9VAASMjllHld8fGn5XkxKhcqMH vVvxhp79jotoOLw-qujm7PnpUwWtRmLLgmhFVxgTqlmFh7Fo y3L~XAIlvgv403cfPTU2ad4DaBW8RTXP~9N1O2oug-9TEMmlEw1 zfuvYr3-2hblTGIR2AiyXk6Geu4T0uttR144uJjF1ftvrlsNoj3XrHug tcd-5XUd5NpC35JutQenuyh5eFSjy95wVAdXmalCa~uxeGd7~8o8 Mvg~BYjdXK95ow__&Key-Pair-Id=APKAJLOHF5GGSLRBV4ZA.

Rambukkana, Nathan. "Sex, space, and discourse: Non/monogamy and intimate privilege in the public sphere." in *Understanding Non-monogamies*, ed. Meg Barker and Darren Langdridge, 237–242. New York: Routledge, 2010.

Rambukkana, Nathan Patrick. "Uncomfortable bridges: The bisexual politics of outing polyamory," *Journal of Bisexuality* 4, no. 3–4 (2004): 141–154.

Rawls, John. *Political Liberalism*. New York: Columbia University Press, 1993.

Rawls, John. "The Idea of Public Reason Revisited." *The University of Chicago Law Review* 64, no. 3 (1997): 765–807.

Raz, Joseph. *The Morality of Freedom* Oxford: Oxford University Press, 1986.

Rickert, Eve, and Carrie Jenkins. "Canada Defines Love—Exclusively (With Carrie Jenkins)." *Medium*, October 31, 2020, https://everickert.medium. com/canada-defines-love-exclusively-63bd57e4ac3d.

Tweedy, Ann E. "Polyamory as a sexual orientation." *University of Cincinnati Law Review* 79 (2010): 1461.

Wlikinson, Eleanor. "What's queer about non-monogamy now," in *Understanding Non-monogamies*, ed. Meg Barker and Darren Langdridge, 243–254. Routledge, 2010.

Five

This book began by pointing out an increasing awareness of, and participation in, non-monogamous relationships. With greater numbers of people encountering non-monogamy for the first time, more and more people have been asking "Is it okay to be non-monogamous?"

I argued that monogamy is a social convention that involves a particular set of beliefs (i.e., romantic relationships are attitude-dependent, dyadic, emotionally, and sexually exclusive). I argued further that non-monogamy cannot be understood independently of monogamy—it is a privative concept that negates at least one, and perhaps all, of the beliefs that constitute monogamy. As a result, non-monogamy includes more than the commonly recognized forms of cheating, swinging, or (increasingly,) polyamory; it also includes lesser-known forms such as friendship and singledom.

Defenders of monogamy, or at least the opponents of non-monogamy, offer a variety of arguments in favor of their position. We saw that these arguments include the *monogamous naturalism argument* (or the belief that monogamy is natural or biological), *divine ordination argument* (or the belief that monogamy's moral status is ordained by God), *the argument from specialness* (or the belief that monogamous relationships are and help us feel special), *the TEA objection* (or the belief that we

DOI: 10.4324/9781003375036-6

do not have unlimited time, energy, and attention to devote to multiple relata), *the argument from sexual health* (or the belief that monogamy helps protect and preserve our sexual health), *arguments about non-monogamous consent* (or the belief that consent performs a kind of "moral magic" for non-monogamists), *the jealousy argument* (or the belief that jealousy provides us with sufficient reasons to avoid being non-monogamous), and *the social fabric argument* (or the belief that non-monogamy, on the whole, is detrimental to the very fabric of society). We also saw that these arguments fall short of showing that non-monogamy is morally impermissible.

The languages that non-monogamists use to describe themselves can be a bit dense because of the nuances they introduce to preserve the distinctiveness of the kind of non-monogamies they participate in. While they might seem confusing initially, we surveyed the ways that "poly" prefixes can still index different non-monogamous practices. For example, *polygamy* (or having multiple *spouses*) is different than *polyamory* (i.e., having multiple loves or having more than one romantic or sexual relationship with the knowledge and consent of all relata involved), *polyfidelity* (a term that non-monogamists use to describe relationships that are based in sexual and emotional fidelity among a group larger than a dyad), *polygyny* (i.e., the practice of having multiple *wives*), and *polyandry* (i.e., the practice of having multiple *husbands*). Among these non-monogamies, we focused on polyamory and showed it to be a morally exemplary kind of non-monogamy. The moral exemplarity of polyamory supports the book's main claim— namely, that it is okay to be non-monogamous.

In addition to being something that people *do*, sometimes monogamy and non-monogamy are used to describe *who people are*. In other words, sometimes monogamy and non-monogamy are taken as kinds of identities. This book suggests that while they are not identities in the most straightforward sense, we can still understand what is meant by folks who describe themselves in this way. Further, I argued that the resulting identity categories create a basis for a non-monogamous political agenda—particularly involving the institution of marriage. Our intimate relationships do not exist in a vacuum; they exist in a wider context of structural inequalities that enhance or stifle our pursuit of a flourishing life. As such, the book ends with a not-so-subtle nudge toward marriage reform.

FOREWORD

1   See the title essay of her *The Right to Sex: Feminism in the Twenty-First Century*
    (New York: Farrar, Straus and Giroux, 2021).
2   See Kim TallBear, *The Critical Polyamorist* blog, www.criticalpolyamorist.
    com/, accessed 9/12/2022.
3   See Friedrich Engels, *The Origin of the Family, Private Property, and the State*,
    ed. Eleanor Burke Leacock (New York: International, 1972) and Emma
    Goldman, *Red Emma Speaks: An Emma Goldman Reader*, ed. Alix Kates Shulman
    (Amherst, NY: Humanity Books, 1998).

WHAT IS NON-MONOGAMY?

1   In July 2020 the Massachusetts city Somerville became the first
    city in the nation to adopt an ordinance recognizing polyamory by
    broadening its definition of domestic partnership to include poly-
    amorous relationships. A year later, in 2021 Cambridge Massachusetts
    became the second city to do so. These events might suggest that a
    turning of the tide might be afoot in the United States.
2   Apryl Alexander, "'We Don't Do That!': Consensual Non-Monogamy in
    HBO's Insecure," *Journal of Black Sexuality and Relationships* 6, no. 2 (2019): 2.
3   C.S.I. Jenkins, "Modal Monogamy," *Ergo, An Open Access Journal of Philosophy*
    no. 2 (2015): 175.
4   John McMurtry, "Monogamy: A Critique," *The Monist* no.4 (October
    1972): 689
5   "Infidelity," American Association for Marriage and Family Therapy,
    accessed December 28, 2021, https://www.aamft.org/Consumer_
    Updates/Infidelity.aspx.
6   More on this point to come later.
7   Some read Shakespeare's Sonnet 116 as implying this conclusion. I am
    grateful to audiences at the "Love" conference in La Crosse, WI for
    pointing this out to me.

8   Diane Enns, *Love in the Dark: Philosophy by another name* (Columbia University Press, 2016), 5; Niko Kolodny, "Love as Valuing a Relationship," *The Philosophical Review* 112, no. 2 (2003): 135–189.

9   Kolodny, "Love as Valuing," 148.

10 Ibid.

11 Danielle Antoinette Hidalgo, Kristen Barber, and Erica Hunter, "The Dyadic Imaginary: Troubling the Perception of Love as Dyadic," *Journal of Bisexuality* 7, no. 3–4 (2008): 173.

12 Ibid.

13 Judith Butler, *Undoing Gender* (New York: Routledge, 2004), 146.

14 Ani Ritchie and Meg Barker, "'There aren't words for what we do or how we feel so we have to make them up': Constructing Polyamorous languages in a culture of compulsory monogamy," *Sexualities* 9, no. 5 (2006): 587.

15 Elizabeth Brake, *Minimizing Marriage: Marriage, morality, and the law* (New York: Oxford University Press 2012), 88.

16 Ibid, 101.

17 Mimi Schippers, *Beyond Monogamy: Polyamory and the future of polyqueer sexualities* (New York: NYU Press); Pepper Mint, "The power dynamics of cheating: Effects on polyamory and bisexuality," *Journal of Bisexuality* 4, no. 3–4 (2004): 55–76.

18 Justin L. Clardy, "Monogamies, Non-Monogamies, and the Moral Impermissibility of Intimacy Confining Constraints," *Journal of Black Sexualities and Relationships* 6, no. 2 (2019): 17–36.

19 More on this later.

20 Nathan Rambukkana, *Fraught Intimacies: Non/monogamy in the public sphere* (British Columbia: UBC Press, 2015); Meg Barker and Darren Langdridge, *Understanding Non-Monogamies* (New York: Routledge, 2010).

21 "Infidelity."

22 Monica T. Whitty, "The realness of cybercheating: Men's and women's representations of unfaithful Internet relationships," *Social Science Computer Review* 23, no. 1 (2005), 57–67.

23 Gary Chartier, "Marriage: A Normative Framework" *Fla. Coastal L. Rev.* 9 (2007): 406.

24 Jessica Fern, *Polysecure: Attachment, Trauma, and Consensual Nonmonogamy* (Portland: Thorntree Press LLC, 2020).

25 Harry Chalmers, "Is Monogamy Morally Permissible?," *Journal of Value Inquiry* 53, no. 2 (2019): 229.

26 Rambukkana, *Fraught Intimacies*, 157.

27 Biondi, Zach, "Open Relationships are for Everybody," Accessed December 30, 2021, https://thevimblog.com/2018/08/26/open-relationships/.

28 Ibid.

29 I am careful here not to mention the rejection of the belief that romantic relationships are attitude dependent as that needn't suggest anything

about one's commitments to monogamous or non-monogamous ideologies. In fact, the belief that relationships are attitude dependent is a metaphysical proposition having to do with the nature of human relationships generally speaking. To reject this proposition is to bring about entailments for one's metaphysics that obscure what kinds of human relationships one might have in mind.

30 Rambukkana, Nathan, and Wilfrid Laurier, "Protecting the Intimate Space of the Nation: Intimacy, Privilege and Canadian Antipolygamy Laws 1892–2012," Accessed December 30, 2021, https://d1wqtxt s1xzle7.cloudfront.net/32348223/Rambukkana_-_Protecting_ the_Intimate_Space_of_the_Nation__SSA13_Talk-with-cover-page-v2.pdf?Expires=1640918036&Signature=YlyPGpAib-uExsiwVfce bHTlFfnce1CCSHXwPQI5RTw-ta06mA-VkMMGwAl0RegCjfSjsiB i3Qe0sWDxAV-mdstG89Zgt0o9VAASMjllHld8fGn5XkxKhcqMH vVvxhp79jotoOLw-qujm7PnpUwWtRmLLgmhFVxgTqlmFh7Fo y3L~XAIlvgv403cfPTU2ad4DaBW8RTXP~9N1O2oug-9TEMmlEw1 zfuvYr3-2hblTGIR2AiyXk6Geu4T0uttR144uJjF1ftvrlsNoj3XrHug tcd-5XUd5NpC35JutQenuyh5eFSjy95wVAdXmalCa~uxeGd7~8o8 Mvg~BYjdXK95ow__&Key-Pair-Id=APKAJLOHF5GGSLRBV4ZA.
31 Ibid.
32 Strauss, Gregg, "Is Polygamy Inherently Unequal?," *Ethics* 122, no. 3 (2012): 517.
33 Under general polygamous ideology, polygyny is the more specific practice of one man having more than one woman spouse. This gets contrasted with polyandry, which is the specific practice of one woman having more than one husband.
34 Ibid, 518.
35 Rambukkana, Nathan, "Open non-monogamies," in *The Palgrave handbook of the psychology of sexuality and gender* (London: Palgrave Macmillan, 2015), 244.
36 Rambukkana, Nathan, *Fraught intimacies: non/monogamy in the public sphere.* (British Columbia: UBC Press, 2015), 28.
37 Ibid, 4.
38 Ibid, 149.
39 Ibid, 15.
40 Mint, Pepper, "The power dynamics of cheating: Effects on polyamory and bisexuality," *Journal of Bisexuality* 4, no. 3–4 (2004): 59.
41 Schippers, Mimi, *Beyond Monogamy: Polyamory and the future of polyqueer sexualities* (New York: NYU Press, 2016), 43.
42 Rambukkana, *Fraught Intimacies*, 16.
43 Berlant, Lauren, *The queen of America goes to Washington City* (Durham: Duke University Press, 1997), 284.
44 Schippers, *Beyond Monogamy*, 43.
45 Rambukkana, *Fraught Intimacies*, 161.
46 Mint, "The Power dynamics of cheating," 58–59.

47 Rambukkana, *Fraught Intimacies*, 58.

48 Klesse, Christian. "Theorizing multi-partner relationships and sexualities—Recent work on non-monogamy and polyamory," *Sexualities* 21, no. 7 (2018): 1119.

49 Rambukkana, *Fraught Intimacies*, 70.

50 Ibid.

51 Ibid, 23.

52 At this point, readers should note that polyamory and polyfidelity are regarded as forms of *ethical* non-monogamy (contrasted to, say adultery and cheating)—however, they may not be the *only* forms of ethical non-monogamy.

53 Ani Ritchie and Meg Barker, "'There aren't words for what we do or how we feel so we have to make them up': Constructing Polyamorous languages in a culture of compulsory monogamy," *Sexualities* 9, no. 5 (2006): 584.

54 Pincus, Tamara, and Rebecca Hiles, *It's Called "Polyamory": Coming Out About Your Nonmonogamous Relationships* (Portland: Thorntree Press LLC, 2017), 6.

55 Sheff, Elisabeth, and Corie Hammers. "The privilege of perversities: Race, class, and education among polyamorists and kinksters," *Psychology & Sexuality* 2, no. 3 (2011): 201.

56 Haritaworn, Jin, Chin-ju Lin, and Christian Klesse, "Poly/logue: A critical introduction to polyamory," *Sexualities* 9, no. 5: 518.

57 Sheff and Hammers, "Privilege Perversities," 201.

58 Ibid.

59 Ibid.

60 Strauss, "Is Polygamy Unequal?," 535.

61 Sheff, Elisabeth, *The polyamorists nextdoor: Inside multiple-partner relationships and families* (Lanham: Rowman & Littlefield, 2015): xiv.

62 Klesse, Christian. *The Spectre of promiscuity: Gay male and bisexual non-monogamies and polyamories* (New York: Routledge, 2016): 109.

63 For one example, in 2019 Organizers of Black Poly Pride drafted a "Meta- Bill of Rights" aimed at establishing best practices for relating to one's metamours—or the partner of one's partner. The document contained normative standards believed to reduce animosity that might be experienced among relata.

64 Rambukkana, *Fraught Intimacies*, 23.

65 Ibid, 24.

66 Harry Chalmers, "Is Monogamy Morally Permissible?," *Journal of Value Inquiry* 53, no. 2 (2019): 229.

67 Brake, *Minimizing Marriage*, 90.

68 Ibid.

69 Ibid, 92.

70 York, Kyle, "Why Monogamy is Morally Permissible: A defense of Some Common Justifications for Monogamy," *The Journal of Value Inquiry* (2019): 1–14.

71 Brake, *Minimizing Marriage*, 95.

72 Ibid, 99–100.

73 Simon, Caroline J, "Just Friends, Friends and Lovers, or...?," *Philosophy and Theology* 8, no. 2 (1993): 113.

74 Clardy, Justin and Alicia-Bunyan Sampson, "Disclosures Vol. 2: Unrecognizable B.U.D.D.Y's," *Medium*, Accessed December 30, 2021, https://urfavfilosopher.medium.com/?p=30c540d91969; Clardy, Justin, "Musings: Romantic Friendships," *Medium*, Accessed December 30, 2021, https://urfavfilosopher.medium.com/musings-romantic-frienships-b3ce02a4d7a7.

75 Brake, *Minimizing Marriage*, 100.

76 Ziegler, Ali, et al., "Monogamy" in *The Palgrave handbook of the psychology of sexuality and gender* (London: Palgrave Macmillan, 2015), 227.

77 Brake, Elizabeth, "Recognizing Care: The case for friendship and poly-amory," *Syracuse Journal of Law and Civic Engagement* 1, no. 1 (2015): 441.

78 DePaulo, Bella, and Bella M. DePaulo, *Singled out: how singles are stereotyped, stigmatized, and ignored, and still live happily ever after* (Macmillan, 2006).

79 Ibid, 210–211.

80 Brake, Elizabeth, *Minimizing marriage: Marriage, morality and the law.* (New York: Oxford University Press, 2011), 92.

81 Ibid, 94.

82 Ibid, 100.

WHY IT'S OK TO NOT BE MONOGAMOUS

1 Séguin, Léa J, "The good, the bad, and the ugly: Lay attitudes and perceptions of polyamory," *Sexualities* 22, no. 4 (2019).

2 Ibid.

3 Ibid, 681.

4 Carrie Jenkins, *What love is: and what it could be*, (New York: Basic Books 2017): 22.

5 Séguin, "The good, the bad."

6 Den Otter, Ronald C, *In defense of plural marriage*, (Cambridge University Press, 2015).

7 George, Robert, Sherif Girgis and Ryan T. Anderson, "The Argument Against Gay Marriage: And Why It Doesn't Fail," Accessed December 30, 2021, www.thepublicdiscourse.com/2010/12/2217/.

8 Goldman, Alan H, "Plain Sex," *Philosophy & Public Affairs* (1977): 267–287.

9 Ibid., 272.

10 What follows in this section is a characterization of a certain view about the moral status of monogamous relationships. I am not concerned with the question of how many philosophers have endorsed this view. Instead, my interest is in targeting a commonplace view that marriage and monogamy have been divinely ordained by God. This argument

is often implicit and assumed even in cases where those who hold it would be unlikely to explicitly declare allegiance to such a position.

11 John McMurtry, "Monogamy: A Critique," *The Monist* no.4 (October 1972): 591.

12 Mt 19:9; Mt 5:2; Lk 12:18.

13 Mt 5:32.

14 Dt 17:17.

15 Plato, "Euthyphro," in *Plato: complete works*, edited by Cooper, John M., and Douglas S. Hutchinson (Indianapolis: Hackett Publishing, 1997), 9.

16 Chalmers, "Is Monogamy Permissible?," 228.

17 Ibid.

18 York, "Monogamy is Permissible," 544.

19 Ibid.

20 Chalmers, "Is Monogamy Permissible?," 237.

21 Ibid., 238.

22 Plato, *"Symposium"* in *Plato: complete works*, edited by Cooper, John M., and Douglas S. Hutchinson (Indianapolis: Hackett Publishing, 1997), 457–505.

23 Chalmers, "Is Monogamy Permissible?," 229.

24 Brunning, Luke, "Compersion: An Alternative to Jealousy?," *Journal of the American Philosophical Association* 6, no. 2 (2020), 226.

25 Chalmers, "Is Monogamy Permissible?," 236.

26 Ibid., 235. The emphasis is my own.

27 Brunning, "Compersion," 230.

28 Chalmers, "Is Monogamy Permissible?," 235.

29 York, "Monogamy is Permissible."

30 Ibid., 548.

31 Ibid., 550.

32 Brunning, "Compersion," 243.

33 Ibid., 226.

34 Ibid.

35 Ibid., 238.

36 Ibid., 231.

37 Ibid., 237.

38 Ibid.

39 Chalmers, "Is Monogamy Permissible?," 236.

40 Ibid., 235.

41 Ibid., 233.

42 Fern, *Polysecure: Attachment, Trauma, and Consensual Nonmonogamy* (Portland: Thorntree Press LLC, 2020).

43 Brunning, "Compersion," 233.

44 Frankfurt, Harry G, *The reasons of Love* (Princeton: Princeton University Press, 2009), 84.

45 York, "Monogamy is Permissible," 541.

46 Ibid.

47 Chalmers, "Is Monogamy Permissible?," 233.

48 Ibid., 232.

49 Jessica Fern, *Polysecure*.

50 Under the actual convention, the amount poured Is differentiated by whether guests request "strong" or "weak" tea. For strong tea requests, hosts are to pour the cup three-fourths full to prevent the tea spilling in to the saucer upon the potential addition of milk, sugar, or lemon. For weak tea requests, hosts are to pour the cup about one-half full, leaving space for the addition of more hot water as a dilutant, and for the potential addition of milk, sugar, or lemon.

51 York, "Monogamy is Permissible," 542.

52 Chalmers, "Is Monogamy Permissible?," 233.

53 I say more about this in Chapter 4.

54 Goldman, Alan H, "Plain Sex," *Philosophy & Public Affairs* (1977): 267–287.

55 Weaver, Bryan R., and Fiona Woollard, "Marriage and the Norm of Monogamy," *The Monist* 91, no. 3–4 (2008): 516.

56 Goldman, "Plain Sex," 285.

57 Ibid., 273.

58 Admittedly, the language of "friends with benefits" is a bit misleading. Colloquially, the "benefits" index the existence of a sexual dimension of a particular relationship. However, friendships just are the kinds of things that people generally benefit from in a variety of ways even when the relationship is not sexual

59 Chalmers, "Is Monogamy Permissible?," 233.

60 York, "Monogamy is Permissible," 543.

61 Marino, *Philosophy of sex and love: an opinionated introduction*. (Routledge, 2019).

62 Marino, *Sex and Love*, 38.

63 Elizabeth Emens, "Monogamy's Law: Compulsory Monogamy and Polyamorous Existence," *NYU Rev. L. & Soc. Change* 29 (2004), 324

64 Marino, *Sex and Love*, 215.

65 Ibid.

66 Ibid.

67 Ibid., 217.

68 Davidson, Joy, "Working with polyamorous clients in the clinical setting," *Electronic Journal of Human Sexuality* 5, no. 8 (2002): 465.

69 Anapol, Deborah M, *Polyamory the new love without limits: Secrets of sustainable intimate relationships*, (IntiNet Resource Center, 1997).

70 Emens, "Monogamy's Law."

71 Bauer, Robin, "Non-Monogamy in Queer BDSM communities: Putting the sex back into alternative relationship practices and discourse," in *Understanding non-monogamies*, ed. Meg Barker and Darren Langdridge (New York: Routledge, 2010), 154–165.

72 Cruz, Ariane, *The Color of Kink*, (New York: NYU Press, 2016).

73 Niko Kolodny, "Love as Valuing a Relationship," *The Philosophical Review* 112, no. 2 (2003): 135–189.

74 Taylor, Gabriele, "Love" in *Proceedings of the Aristotelian Society* 76, no. 1 (1976).

75 Pineau, Lois, "Date rape: A feminist analysis," *Law and Philosophy* 8, no. 2 (1989): 217–243.

76 Broadie, Sarah, and Christopher Rowe, eds. *Nicomachean Ethics* (New York: Oxford University Press, 2002), 117.

77 Diane Enns, *Love in the Dark: Philosophy by another name* (Columbia University Press, 2016).

78 Anderson, Michelle J, "Negotiating Sex," *S. Cal. L. Rev.* 78 (2005): 101.

79 Ibid., 122.

80 Strauss, Gregg, "Is Polygamy Inherently Unequal?," *Ethics* 122, no. 3 (2012).

81 Ibid, 517.

82 D/S stands for the dynamics of domination-submission sexual behaviors associated with BDSM and Kink communities and practitioners.

83 Samuels, Andrew, "Promiscuities: Politics, imagination, spirituality and hypocrisy," in *Understanding non-monogamies*, ed. Meg Barker and Darren Langdridge (New York: Routledge, 2010).

84 Cruz, *The Color of Kink*.

85 Den Otter, *In defense of plural marriage*, 122.

86 Rickert, Eve, "Can Polyamorous hierarchies be ethical? Part 1: The tower and the village," Accessed December 31, 2021, https://brighterthansunflowers.com/2016/06/10/can-polyamorous-hierarchies-ethical-part-1-tower-village/.

87 Ibid.

88 Samuels, "Promiscuities".

89 Sheff, Elisabeth, *The polyamorists nextdoor: Inside multiple-partner relationships and families* (Lanham: Rowman & Littlefield, 2015): 262.

90 Séguin, "The good, the bad."

91 Sheff, Elisabeth, *The polyamorists nextdoor*, xi.

92 Ibid.

93 Ibid.

94 Wlikinson, Eleanor, "What's queer about non-monogamy now," in *Understanding non-monogamies*, ed. Meg Barker and Darren Langdridge (New York: Routledge, 2010), 252.

95 Sheff, Elisabeth, *The polyamorists nextdoor*, 242.

96 Ibid, 275.

97 Den Otter, *In defense of plural marriage*, 148.

98 Ibid, 147.

99 Ibid, 137.

100 We should also note here that for Kant, monogamy and not polygamy is morally permissible because in the case of polygyny, "each wife

would have half a husband, since she has given herself to him, and thus has a total right to a person as well." (27:389).

101 Readers should note that some scholars do not think that the formula of the universal law is not a 'universalizability test' so to speak.

MONOGAMOUS AND NON-MONOGAMOUS IDENTITY

1 Ann E. Tweedy, "Polyamory as a Sexual Orientation," *U. Cin. L. Rev.* 79 (2010); Christine Overall, "Monogamy, nonmonogamy, and identity," *Hypatia* 13, no. 4 (1998); Elizabeth Emens, "Monogamy's Law: Compulsory Monogamy and Polyamorous Existence," *NYU Rev. L. & Soc. Change* 29 (2004).

2 Ritchie and Barker, "'There aren't words for what we do or how we feel so we have to make them up': Constructing Polyamorous languages in a culture of compulsory monogamy," *Sexualities* 9, no. 5 (2006).

3 Tweedy, "Polyamory as"; John Witte Jr., *The Western case for monogamy over polygamy* (New York: Cambridge University Press, 2015).

4 Carrie Jenkins and Eve Rickert, "Canada Defines Love—Exclusively (With Carrie Jenkins)," *Medium*, October 31, 2020, https://everickert.medium.com/canada-defines-love-exclusively-63bd57e4ac3d.

5 Carrie Jenkins, *What love is: and what it could be*, (New York: Basic Books 2017); Justin L. Clardy, "'I Don't Want To be a Playa No More': An Exploration of 'Player' as a Stereotype Against African American Polyamorous Men," *AnALize: Revista de studii feminist* 11, no. 25 (2018); Justin L. Clardy, "Toward a progressive black sexual politics: reading African American Polyamorous Women in Patricia Hill Collins' Black Feminist Thought," in *Routledge Companion to Romantic Love* (New York: Routledge, 2021), 153–161; Patricia Hill Collins, *Black Feminist Thought: Knowledge, consciousness, and the politics of empowerment* (New York: Routledge 2000), 69–96.

6 Tweedy, "Polyamory as," 1482.

7 Samuel Macrosson, "Constructive immutability," *U. Pa. J. Const. L.* 3 (2001), 682.

8 Tweedy, "Polyamory as," 1482.

9 Tweedy, "Polyamory as," 1483.

10 There may be some questions here about whether an identity could be embedded and non-resonant, or further whether something a set of beliefs could be deeply resonant for an individual that does not take up a particular identity. I address the latter question in the text. Regarding the former, it is appropriate to wonder about the possibility of identities that are experienced as embedded despite lacking resonance with the belief set. Exploring this question fully would take us too far afield here. Suffice it to say that in cases like these a particular kind of dissonance in/with oneself is likely to result. What should be said of

the identity of the person who experiences this dissonance is an open question to be explored in future research.

11 The language here is careful to be inclusive to the possibility that people may be self-deceived about their beliefs in the case that their actions do not align with what they take themselves to believe. Ultimately, how this story is told will likely depend on whether one is an internalist or an externalist about motivation for human action.

12 Emens, "Monogamy's Law," 284.

13 Brake, *Minimizing Marriage*, 159.

14 At the time of this writing, it can be said with some confidence that this tide is beginning to turn in non-monogamists favor. In recent years there has been a proliferation of representation of different forms of non-monogamy including the TV shows like *She's Gotta Have It*, *Sister Wives*, *Big Love*, *Trigonometry* and feature films such as *Supafly or Ma Belle, My Beauty*. This media, when taken as a whole, presents a broad spectrum of permissible forms of ethical non-monogamy.

15 Jenkins, *What Love is*.

16 Ann E. Tweedy, "Polyamory as a Sexual Orientation," *U. Cin. L. Rev.* 79 (2010)

17 Ritchie and Barker, "There aren't words," 585.

18 Ibid.

19 Ibid.

20 Ibid.

21 Ibid, 587.

22 Weeks, Jeffrey, *Sexuality* (London: Routledge, 2003).

23 Ritchie and Barker, "There aren't words," 590.

24 See Elizabeth Emens, "Monogamy's Law: Compulsory Monogamy and Polyamorous Existence," *NYU Rev. L. & Soc. Change* 29 (2004).

25 Tweedy, "Polyamory as," 1483.

26 Rambukkana, Nathan Patrick. "Uncomfortable bridges: The bisexual politics of outing polyamory," *Journal of Bisexuality* 4, no. 3–4 (2004): 141–154.

27 Tweedy, "Polyamory as," 1486.

WHY IT'S NOT OK FOR LIBERAL STATES
TO BE MONOGAMOUS

1 Apryl Alexander, "'We Don't Do That!': Consensual Non-Monogamy in HBO's Insecure," *Journal of Black Sexuality and Relationships* 6, no.2 (2019): 2.

2 Anapol, Deborah M, *Polyamory the new love without limits: Secrets of sustainable intimate relationships* (IntiNet Resource Center, 1997), 44.

3 Den Otter, Ronald C, *In defense of plural marriage* (Cambridge University Press, 2015).

4 Carrie Jenkins and Eve Rickert, "Canada Defines Love—Exclusively (With Carrie Jenkins)," *Medium*, October 31, 2020, https://everickert. medium.com/canada-defines-love-exclusively-63bd57e4ac3d.

5 Elizabeth Brake, *Minimizing Marriage: Marriage, morality, and the law* (New York: Oxford University Press 2012).

6 Raz, Joseph, *The Morality of Freedom* (Oxford: Oxford University Press, 1986).

7 Devlin, Patrick, *The Enforcement of Morals* (Oxford: Oxford University Press, 1965).

8 Rawls, John, "The Idea of Public Reason Revisited," *The University of Chicago Law Review* 64, no. 3 (1997), 766.

9 Brake, *Minimizing Marriage*, 136.

10 Rawls, John, *Political Liberalism*, (New York: Columbia University Press, 1993): 192–193.

11 See Especially Wlikinson, Eleanor, "What's queer about non-monogamy now," in *Understanding non-monogamies*, ed. Meg Barker and Darren Langdridge (New York: Routledge, 2010); and Brake, Elizabeth, "Equality and non-hierarchy in marriage: what do feminists really want?," in *After Marriage: Rethinking Marital Relationships* ed. Elizabeth Brake (New York: Oxford University Press, 2016).

12 May, Simon Cābuela, "Liberal Neutrality and Civil Marriage," in *After Marriage: Rethinking Marital Relationships* ed. Elizabeth Brake (New York: Oxford University Press, 2016), 9–28.

13 Rawls, "Public Reason."

14 Ibid., 779.

15 De Marneffe, Peter, "Liberty and Polygamy," in *After Marriage: Rethinking Marital Relationships* ed. Elizabeth Brake (New York: Oxford University Press, 2016), 125–159.

16 Ibid., 149.

17 Brake, *Minimizing Marriage*, 61.

18 De Marneffe, "Liberty."

19 Elizabeth Emens, "Monogamy's Law: Compulsory Monogamy and Polyamorous Existence," *NYU Rev. L. & Soc. Change* 29 (2004), 279.

20 Case, Mary Anne, "Marriage Licenses," *Minn. L. Rev.* 89 (2004): 1758.

21 Rambukkana, Nathan, and Wilfrid Laurier, "Protecting the Intimate Space of the Nation: Intimacy, Privilege and Canadian Antipolygamy Laws 1892–2012," Accessed December 30, 2021, https://d1wqtxt s1xzle7.cloudfront.net/32348223/Rambukkana_-_Protecting_ the_Intimate_Space_of_the_Nation__SSA13_Talk-with-cover-page-v2.pdf?Expires=1640918036&Signature=YlyPGpAib-uExsiwVfce bHTlFfnce1CCSHXwPQI5RTw-ta06mA-VkMMGwAl0RegCjfSjsiB i3Qe0sWDxAV-mdstG89Zgt0o9VAASMjllHld8fGn5XkxKhcqMH vVvxhp79jotoOLw-qujm7PnpUwWtRmLLgmhFVxgTqlmFh7Fo y3L~XAIlvgv403cfPTU2ad4DaBW8RTXP~9N1O2oug-9TEMmlEw1 zfuvYr3-2hblTGIR2AiyXk6Geu4T0uttR144uJjF1ftvrlsNoj3XrHug tcd-5XUd5NpC35JutQenuyh5eFSjy95wVAdXmalCa~uxeGd7~8o8 Mvg~BYjdXK95ow__&Key-Pair-Id=APKAJLOHF5GGSLRBV4ZA.

22 Emens, "Monogamy's law."; Ann E. Tweedy, "Polyamory as a Sexual Orientation," *U. Cin. L. Rev.* 79 (2010).; Goring, Darlene C, "The history of slave marriage in the United States," *J. Marshall L. Rev.* 39 (2005), 299.

23 Den Otter, *Plural Marriage*, 32.

24 Den Otter, *Plural Marriage*, 34.

25 Karimi, Faith, "Three dads, a baby, and the legal battle to get their names added to a birth certificate," Accessed December 31, 2021, www.cnn.com/2021/03/06/us/throuple-three-dads-and-baby-trnd/index.html

26 Rambukkana, Nathan, "Sex, space, and discourse: Non/monogamy and intimate privilege in the public sphere," in *Understanding non-monogamies*, ed. Meg Barker and Darren Langdridge (New York: Routledge, 2010), 237–242.

27 Den Otter, *Plural Marriage*, 50.

28 Ibid.

29 Wlikinson, "What's Queer."; Rambukkana, Nathan Patrick. "Uncomfortable bridges: The bisexual politics of outing polyamory," *Journal of Bisexuality* 4, no. 3–4 (2004): 141–154.

30 Aviram, Hadar, "Geeks, goddesses, and green eggs: Political mobilization and the cultural locus of the polyamorous community in the San Francisco Bay Area," in *Understanding non-monogamies*, ed. Meg Barker and Darren Langdridge (New York: Routledge, 2010), 99–105.

31 Emens, "Monogamy's Law," see footnote 316.

32 Ibid, see footnote 415.

33 Karimi, "Three dads."

34 Den Otter, *Plural Marriage*, 42.

35 Ibid., 43.

36 Emens, "Monogamy's Law," 350.

37 Tweedy, "Polyamory As," 1514.

38 Davis, Angela Y., *Are Prisons obsolete?* (New York: Seven Stories Press, 2011).

39 McLeod, Allegra M., "Confronting Criminal Law's Violence: The Possibilities of Unfinished Alternatives," *Harvard Unbound* 8, (2013): 109–132.

40 Brake, *Minimizing Marriage*, 31.

41 Brake notes that this "includes both polyfidelity—sexual exclusivity within the group—and open relationships in which primary partners have secondary relationships with others."

42 Brake, Elizabeth, "Recognizing Care: The case for friendship and polyamory," *Syracuse Journal of Law and Civic Engagement* 1, no. 1 (2015): 441.

43 Brake, *Minimizing Marriage*, 157.

44 Ibid, 156.

45 Ibid, 158.

46 Ibid, 159.

47 In her list, Brake includes benefits such as evidentiary spousal privilege in criminal law cases and prison visitation rights. I am careful to omit these here as it is far from clear whether an ideal egalitarian society

includes prisons or a criminal justice system altogether. A tradition of prison abolitionists including Angela Davis and others, challenge this very assumption.

48 Brake, "Recognizing Care."
49 Rambukkana, "Uncomfortable Bridges."
50 Wilkinson, "What's Queer."
51 Cherry, Myisha, *The Case for Rage: Why Anger Is Essential to Anti-Racist Struggle* (New York: Oxford University Press, 2021); Nussbaum, Martha C., *Political emotions* (Harvard: Harvard University Press, 2013); Clardy Justin Leonard, "Civic Tenderness as a Response to Child Poverty in America," in *Philosophy and Child Poverty* ed. Nicolás Brando and Gottfried Schweiger (Springer Nature, 2019), 303–320.
52 Brake, "Recognizing Care."
53 Ibid.
54 Den Otter, *Plural Marriage*, 34.
55 Brake, "Recognizing Care."
56 Brake, *Minimizing Marriage*, 163.
57 Emens, "Monogamy's Law."
58 Brake, *Minimizing Marriage*, 186.

Printed in the United States
by Baker & Taylor Publisher Services